Scripture and Sport Psychology

Scripture and Sport Psychology

◆

Mental-Game Techniques for the Christian Athlete

Derek de la Peña, Ph.D.

iUniverse, Inc.
New York Lincoln Shanghai

Scripture and Sport Psychology
Mental-Game Techniques for the Christian Athlete

All Rights Reserved © 2004 by Derek de la Peña

No part of this book may be reproduced or transmitted in any form or by any means, graphic, electronic, or mechanical, including photocopying, recording, taping, or by any information storage retrieval system, without the written permission of the publisher.

iUniverse, Inc.

For information address:
iUniverse, Inc.
2021 Pine Lake Road, Suite 100
Lincoln, NE 68512
www.iuniverse.com

Scripture quotations are taken from the Holy Bible, New Living Translation, copyright © 1996. Used by permission of Tyndale House Publishers, Inc., Wheaton, Illinois 60189. All rights reserved.

ISBN: 0-595-32833-4

Printed in the United States of America

Contents

ACKNOWLEDGMENTS ....*ix*

PREFACE ....*xi*

INTRODUCTION 1

SECTION I: BUILDING SELF-CONFIDENCE 3
   Introduction
   Lesson 1: Practice Like You Play, and Play Like You Practice 5
   Application: Lesson 1 7
   Lesson 2: Positive Self-Talk 9
   Application: Lesson 2 11
   Lesson 3: Mental Imagery 13
   Application: Lesson 3 15
   Lesson 4: Expect Good Things to Happen 17
   Application: Lesson 4 19
   Lesson 5: Modeling 21
   Application: Lesson 5 23
   Lesson 6: Anxiety Can Help Performance 25
   Application: Lesson 6 27
   Review of Main Points: Building Self-Confidence 29
   References: Building Self-Confidence 31

SECTION II: PURPOSE, MOTIVATION, ATTITUDE,
AND GOALS 33
   Introduction
   Lesson 1: Purpose—Why do You Play? 35

Lesson 2: Motivation 37

Attitude—Introduction (Lessons 3-6) 39

Lesson 3: Attitude—Patience and Sportsmanship 41

Lesson 4: Attitude and What Love is Not 43

Lesson 5: Attitude and Forgiveness 45

Lesson 6: Attitude and Endurance 47

Lesson 7: Goal-setting Philosophy 49

Application: Lesson 7 51

Lesson 8: Goal-setting Process 53

Application: Lesson 8 55

Review of Main Points: Purpose, Motivation, Attitude, and Goals 57

References: Purpose, Motivation, Attitude, and Goals 59

SECTION III: DEALING WITH ADVERSITY 60

Introduction

Lesson 1: Adversity is Part of the Game 62

Application: Lesson 1 64

Lesson 2: Worry and Prayer 66

Application: Lesson 2 68

Lesson 3: Patience and Adversity 70

Application: Lesson 3 72

Lesson 4: Negative Peer Pressure 74

Lesson 5: Criticism 76

Application: Lesson 5 78

Lesson 6: Slumping and Rest 80

Lesson 7: Injuries 82

Application: Lesson 7 84

Review of Main Points: Dealing with Adversity 86

References: Dealing with Adversity 88

SECTION IV: PLAYING IN THE ZONE 90
Introduction
Lesson 1: Stay in the Present 92
Application: Lesson 1 94
Lesson 2: Faith 96
Lesson 3: Rules of the Task 98
Lesson 4: Hard Work 100
Application: Lessons 2-4 102
Lesson 5: Enjoy the Moment 106
Application: Lesson 5 107
Review of Main Points: Playing in the Zone 109
References: Playing in the Zone 111

SECTION V: TEAMWORK 113
Introduction
Lesson 1: Serve Your Team, Not Yourself 115
Application: Lesson 1 117
Lesson 2: Understanding and Accepting Your Role on the Team 119
Application: Lesson 2 121
Lesson 3: Cohesion Versus Conflict 123
Application: Lesson 3 125
Lesson 4: Player/Coach Relationship 127
Application: Lesson 4 129
Review of Main Points: Teamwork 131
References: Teamwork 134

CONCLUSION *135*

GLOSSARY *137*

ACKNOWLEDGMENTS

I would like to thank several people for their help with this book. First and foremost, I would like to thank my Lord and Savior Jesus Christ for giving me the ability to read, write, and play sports. Thank you for providing me with everything I need to be happy. Without you in my life, I am nothing. Next, I would like to thank my wonderful wife Merida for editing this book—it certainly was a pleasure working with you. You are the smartest, prettiest, and sweetest woman I know. I am truly blessed to have you in my life. I would also like to thank Pastor Casey Jones, Dr. Chris Janelle, and my mother Jane. I thank each of you for your feedback, encouragement, and edits to this book. I would like to thank the rest of my family and friends for all of the love and support you have always given me. Because of you, my life is full of joy. Finally, a special thank you to all the Christian athletes who play sports with a love for Jesus Christ—you were the inspiration for this book.

PREFACE

This book was created for the Christian athlete. If you are not yet a Christian or if you would describe yourself as a "seeker," you are welcome to read this book, but it was primarily written for those who already have devoted themselves to Jesus Christ as Lord and Savior.

The book began in the fall of 1997 when I entered graduate school at the University of Florida as a sport psychology doctoral student. On a number of occasions during my studies, I noticed themes from the Bible that seemed to relate to concepts I learned about in sport psychology literature. I kept a file of notes over the next four years that in my mind could be potentially useful for Christian athletes from a spiritual and mental-game standpoint.

The words "Scripture and Sport Psychology" in the title of the book were purposely placed in that order to emphasize the importance of the Bible coming first. In my opinion, the Bible is the most important book anyone could ever read. I also believe that trying to understand and apply the teachings of Jesus Christ should be a primary objective for all Christians. If your intention with sports is to be the best <u>Christian athlete</u> you can be, then you must stay close to Jesus Christ and you must have a sound mental-game. My goal has been to create a book that offers simple techniques to help with these objectives.

When I reached the end of my graduate school tenure I realized how blessed I was to receive a wonderful education. I felt in my heart that there was a way the lessons I learned from the Bible and from my books in graduate school could be united systematically to help Christian athletes improve their mental-game, and ultimately, their sport performance. When I graduated in the summer of 2001, I made a promise to myself that I would write this book. I hope you find it helpful.

INTRODUCTION

"…'You must love the Lord your God with all your heart, all your soul, and all your mind.' This is the first and greatest commandment. A second is equally important: 'Love your neighbor as yourself.' All the other commandments and all the demands of the prophets are based on these two commandments." Matthew 22:37-40

Congratulations! You are a Christian athlete. How lucky you are to be blessed with the ability to play sports. Because you believe and trust in Christ, you are saved, and no matter how much success playing sports has brought or will bring you, the most important achievement in your life has already been accomplished—YOU CHOSE TO BELIEVE AND RECEIVE JESUS CHRIST!

The purpose of this book is two-fold. The primary objective is to bring you closer to Jesus Christ. Sports can play a wonderful role in your life, especially when Jesus comes first. Enhancing your relationship with Jesus Christ is the primary purpose of this book. The next objective is to help you with your mental-game from a Christian perspective. Without a strong mental-game, your potential as an athlete is limited. This book draws on enlightening parallels from the Bible (New Living Translation) and sport psychology literature research to provide you with effective techniques to develop the mental fortitude necessary for you to perform your best. The sections of the book are: 1. Building Confidence, 2. Purpose, Motivation, Attitude, and Goals, 3. Dealing with Adversity, 4. Playing in the Zone, and 5. Being a Team Player.

Keep in mind that no matter which techniques you choose to use or not to use, the most important belief to practice is quoted above in **Matthew 22:37-40**. To be a truly confident Christian, you must follow Christ. Without him in your life, sports do not really matter. You can be sure that someday you will have to leave sports behind. But because you believe and trust in Jesus Christ, he will never leave you. With him, you can never lose in life!

As an athlete, if you love Jesus with all of your heart and are able to treat your teammates, coaches, and even opponents as you would want to be treated then the stage will be set for sports to play a wonderful role in your life. My hope is that this book will help guide you through your journey as a Christian athlete.

Suggested Prayer: "Lord Jesus, please help me to put you first in my life and help me to love you as much as you love me. Also, help me to treat others as I would like to be treated. Amen."

SECTION I: BUILDING SELF-CONFIDENCE

"O LORD, you are my light; yes, LORD, you light up my darkness. In your strength I can crush an army; with my God I can scale any wall." 2 Samuel 22:29-30

Self-confidence has been frequently cited as the most important determinant of sport performance. ***Self-confidence*** is the general belief that one has the ability to perform successfully.[1] Think of self-confidence as a "building" that needs to be built and maintained. The raw materials will be the techniques discussed in this section. Your goal is to build and maintain as big and strong of a building as possible. It takes time to build an impressive building, so do not expect to achieve a high degree of confidence overnight. God gives each of us the potential to have a big and strong building, but he wants to watch us build it! Keep in mind that Christ wants you to build it gracefully. Never let arrogance be part of the process.

Research has demonstrated that several factors contribute to self-confidence. The most important factor is your performance. When you are performing well in practice and in competition, you will feel

---

1. Reference citations for footnotes throughout the book can be found at the end of each respective section.

more confident than when you are struggling. Therefore, it is imperative that you work hard in practice to help ensure that your performance will be good when it counts. Other factors contribute to confidence to a lesser degree, such as how you talk to yourself during competition, your ability to be optimistic, your body language, and how you interpret feelings of nervousness. Although these factors are not as influential as performance, they are still important materials to your confidence building. In this section, in addition to emphasizing the importance of hard work, several techniques will be discussed that can help make your building as solid as possible. These techniques include positive self-talk, mental imagery, situational favorableness, modeling, and the positive interpretation of anxiety symptoms.

When you play, some days will be stormy, some will not. Some days "lady luck" will appear to be on your side, some days she will not. Keep in mind that <u>building</u> confidence is a process and your building will never be finished. The winds and rains of sport will constantly knock bricks out—be ready to keep replacing them! Remember, with God you can "scale any wall." Be sure the walls of your confidence building are as big and strong as possible to prevent the inclement weather of sport from knocking them down.

Lesson 1—PRACTICE LIKE YOU PLAY, AND PLAY LIKE YOU PRACTICE

"Work hard so God can approve you. Be a good worker, one who does not need to be ashamed and who correctly explains the word of truth." 2 Timothy 2:15

Because the key ingredient to confidence is performance, it is important that you <u>work hard during practice sessions</u>. Practice is when the foundation of your confidence will be built. Commit to the creed "<u>practice like you play, and play like you practice</u>." Remember that each time you perform a task successfully, it slowly contributes to building your confidence. When you are successful at a particular task over and over again in practice, you will begin to believe that you can perform the task effectively when it counts. Be sure to give it your <u>best effort</u> when you practice. Practice in a way that is characteristic of a champion—never forget, preparation will serve as the foundation to your confidence! The harder you work during practice the more you will believe that the prize will be yours.

> "Remember that in a race everyone runs, but only one person gets the prize. You also must run in such a way that you will win." 1 Corinthians 9:24

Unfortunately, some athletes do not try their best in practice because they think it is a waste of energy. Some might not give it their best effort against teammates because they do not want to make themselves or another teammate look bad. It is important for teammates to understand that the easier they make it for each other, the less confident they will be against strong competition. Do not think of sanctioned competition as the only time performance counts. Deep down inside yourself, you will know that your confidence foundation is not very strong if you did not commit to giving it your best during practice. If you work hard during practice sessions and eventually master certain skills, you will have the potential to perform even better when people are watching. Think of God as watching you, every time you practice. Therefore, **"[w]ork hard so God can approve you…" 2 Timothy 2:15.** Then, when it is gametime, think of it as just another day at work, it is time to play like you practiced!

APPLICATION—Practice Like You Play, and Play Like You Practice

Suggested Prayer: "Lord Jesus, please help me to work hard today in a way that would be pleasing to you. Be with me as I give it my best. I need you more than anything in the world. Amen."

As mentioned in the introduction to this section, building your confidence is a process, it will not happen overnight. You are responsible for building your building of confidence, and Jesus will watch you build it. He will always know when you give it your best, and this is what he wants from you. You should want to impress him the most.

Although performance during games and practice is what ultimately contributes the most to your confidence, you can't always control the results of your performance. Jesus understands this, and will not be disappointed with you if you do not perform your best, as long as you give it your <u>best effort</u>. Remember, you CAN control the effort you give each day. Knowing that you gave it your best, with the motive to please God first is really all you can ask of yourself.

Now that the importance of effort has been emphasized, how will you monitor whether you give it your best effort on a day to day basis? Giving one's best effort during games is usually not a problem, but giving 100% during practice is not always easy—this is what you should monitor. An effective technique is to "pay yourself" for your efforts after each practice.[2] Find a jar and label it "Practice Salary." Pick an amount of money that will symbolize your best effort, for example, a quarter. After each practice, if you can look back and honestly say to yourself that you gave it your best effort, then put a quarter in the jar. Do not give yourself anything less. That is, do not give yourself twenty cents if you gave it 80% of your effort. You either earned the quarter or you didn't. Calculate how many practice days you will have during the season and then make a goal to raise a certain amount of money. Commit to that amount and give it your best each day to earn your wages. Remember, you CAN control the effort you give—commit to giving it your best!

Lesson 2—POSITIVE SELF-TALK

"…I can do everything with the help of Christ who gives me the strength I need." Philippians 4:13

How good of a self-coach are you? In order to be a confident athlete, you must be an effective self-coach who engages in positive self-talk, particularly when things are not going your way. *Self-talk* is how you talk to yourself before, during, and after your performance.[3] Positive self-talk is the use of constructive language to direct or assess performance. Talking to yourself is <u>not</u> an abnormal behavior. In fact, every professional athlete talks to his or herself to some degree. We all get down on ourselves from time to time, but we must have the ability to pick ourselves up. Coaches, families, and friends can be excellent teachers and counselors, but ultimately, you are the biggest influence when it comes to how you think of yourself. In order to achieve and maintain confidence, you must commit to being the best self-coach you can be. For these reasons, positive self-talk is a skill that needs to be developed.

Positive self-talk is a useful technique that should be used during practice, games, and even everyday life. With regard to sport, positive self-talk is effective before and after the execution of a particular skill. It is especially important to be positive after performing poorly. When athletes perform well, they usually talk to themselves in a positive way. However, it is when performance is not up to par that your ability as a self-coach is crucial. Constantly criticizing yourself will ultimately chip away at your confidence. You have a choice when it comes to how you assess yourself. When you are not playing well, remember to trust Jesus first, and know that he is with you. Christ wants you to trust in yourself, and you will need self-trust in order to play your best. In order to fully trust in yourself, you need to talk to yourself in a way that is constructive. In the application that follows, an effective approach to self-talk is discussed. No matter which phrases of self-talk you choose to use, perhaps the best example of self-talk that can be practiced anytime is quoted above in **Philippians 4:13**—remind yourself of this constantly!

APPLICATION: Positive Self-Talk

Suggested Prayer: "Lord Jesus, help me to trust in you first and in myself second. Help me to be the best self-coach I can be. When I don't perform the way I would like, help me to talk to myself in a constructive way. Amen."

If you haven't already done so, find a notebook so that you can jot down notes to help you apply the lessons in this book. Write this question down, "*When I am playing poorly, do I assess my behavior in a judgmental or descriptive way?*" Next, think about the concept of being judgmental versus being descriptive. The following quotes are examples of being judgmental, "that was pathetic!", "you stink!", or "you choked again!" Notice that with each of these examples, a negative judgment of the performance was made. Now consider the following descriptive examples, "you pulled that shot", "you took your eye off the ball", or "you hurried that one." With each of these examples, a personal judgment was not made, but rather, what took place was simply described.

In order to be the best self-coach you can be, you must choose to describe and correct your behavior and avoid being judgmental.[4] Judgmental thinking promotes a mentality geared towards avoiding failure. Ponder the following statement for a few seconds, "don't mess up again." When an athlete's mind is focused primarily on what not to do, a common result is a timid performance. It is safe to say that you will never reach your potential if you are timid when you perform. Remember this, a good self-coach does not focus on avoiding failure, a good self-coach focuses on what needs to be done in order to execute effectively. A good self-coach assesses and corrects, and avoids being judgmental. For example, "you took your eyes off the ball, keep your head down next time", or "you hurried that one, take your time." In each of these examples, a descriptive assessment was made, followed by a correcting instruction. No judgments were made nor was the focus on what not to do. In the future, if you find that your self-talk is negative, commit to being more constructive—<u>describe and correct</u>! Whenever you assess your mental-game, always give yourself a grade on the quality of your self-talk. You can be sure that over time, the better grades you make, the more confident you will be.

Lesson 3—MENTAL IMAGERY

"...Fix your thoughts on what is true and honorable and right. Think about things that are pure and lovely and admirable. Think about things that are excellent and worthy of praise." Philippians 4:8

Another technique that is helpful for confidence is mental imagery. *Mental Imagery* is the act of seeing and/or feeling the skill that you hope to perform before actually doing it.[5] Imagery can serve several purposes, but two of the most important functions are to "prime" your muscles for the impending action, and to foster an optimistic mind-set.[6] Consider the following examples. Just before performing, a platform diver visualizes in her "mind's eye" herself executing the perfect "two and a half with a twist" with minimal splash at entry. While standing in the batter's box, a baseball player visualizes himself putting the barrel of the bat on an incoming fastball. Just before an important race, a runner feels stomach "butterflies." However, he interprets his nervous feelings as positive and images himself running an awesome race in spite of his feelings. With each of these examples, imagery was used to help foster an optimistic mind-set and get the athlete's body ready for action.

Remember that Christ wants you to focus your attention on positive thoughts. Although it is not possible to know exactly what kind of thoughts Jesus would consider "worthy of praise," commit to making your thoughts as optimistic as possible. Sometimes the mind of an athlete wanders to thoughts and images that are characterized by negative performance. This is not uncommon, as everyone fears failure to some degree. However, it is important to know that you can be proactive with your thinking. <u>Do not</u> let your mind "think on its own"—be sure that you are the pilot of your thoughts and images. Fill your mind with pictures of success! Remember that the purpose of imagery is to get your mind and body ready to perform in an effective manner. If you don't get the hit you imaged or run the race that you envisioned, don't give up on yourself or the imagery strategy, but rather, image how you will bounce back and prepare for the next opportunity. Don't forget, imagery can help your confidence when you image in a way that fosters optimism!

APPLICATION: Mental Imagery

Suggested Prayer: "Lord Jesus, when I play, let my mind be filled with images of success. Help me to focus on images that are worthy of praise. Amen."

In your notebook, write this question down, *"When and how should I use mental imagery?"* Take some time to think about the question as it pertains to your sport. No matter which sport you play, mental imagery can help with pre-competition preparation. There are many ways to image in the hours before you perform. One way is to use deep breathing, then pray, then image. Practice the following exercise. First, find a place that is as quiet as possible. If you find it to be too noisy around you, a useful technique is to use headphones with some music that helps you relax. Take deep, slow breaths through your nose while concentrating on filling your lungs up with air and slowly emptying them. Do this for a few minutes until you feel more relaxed. Then, focus on the *suggested prayer*. Once you have finished praying, pause for a moment of silence, then concentrate on the objectives of your particular sport. See yourself performing in a way that you know you can. See yourself giving it your best effort even if adversities come your way.

In addition to being useful before competition, imagery can also help with confidence if it is used during and after competition. With tasks such as hitting a golf ball, serving a tennis ball, or pitching a baseball, the individual has time to image just before executing the movement—so imagery can be used throughout the competition. Techniques to use during competition will be discussed in Section IV (Playing in the Zone). For now, practice using imagery after competition in addition to before it. Following a performance in which you performed well, take a couple of minutes to focus on the images of success that occurred. In other words, focus on the things that you did well. Always focus on what you did well first, even following disappointing performances. If you are not happy with your performance, visualize how you plan to correct your mistakes for next time. Remember, always try to image in a way that Jesus would approve—in a way he might consider "worthy of praise."

Lesson 4—EXPECT GOOD THINGS TO HAPPEN

"So I pray that God, who gives you hope, will keep you happy and full of peace as you believe in him. May you overflow with hope through the power of the Holy Spirit." Romans 15:13

An old technique for measuring optimism is filling a glass halfway with water and then asking, "Is the glass half full, or half empty?" If an individual answers "half full" then this person is presumed by some to have a more optimistic personality than an individual who answers "half empty." In sports, individuals who possess a high degree of ***situational favorableness*** are those who tend to believe that the breaks of a sporting situation are going, or will eventually go, in their favor.[7] These types of individuals are likely to see the glass "half full" and expect good things to happen regardless of the situation. You have a choice in how you interpret the way things are going. Even when things are obviously not going your way, it is important to be optimistic that things will eventually turn around. Athletes who tend to focus too much on what is going wrong with their particular game situation, will never be as confident as they can be.

In sports and in life there will be situations you can control and others you cannot. It is important to assume that you have an "internal locus of control" over competitive situations until proven otherwise. To have an ***internal locus of control*** means that an individual believes that he or she can control the outcome of a given situation. Conversely, one who has an ***external locus of control*** believes that little or no relationship exists between one's actions and the outcome of the situation. Research generally indicates that "internal" individuals are more productive and achieve more in life.[8] Yes, Jesus has a glorious plan for us all and he has the final say in every outcome—some situations and outcomes we will not be able to control. However, it is safe to assume that Christ wants us to be as proactive as we can to make great things happen.

> **"Dear brothers and sisters, what's the use of saying you have faith if you don't prove it by your actions?" James 2:14**

Jesus doesn't want us to just sit back and watch life go by. He wants us to be hopeful and proactive! Expect good things to happen and assume that your actions will bring about success. Remember, Christ wants you to be hopeful no matter if things are going your way or not. Losing will never bring you shame as a Christian as long as you put Jesus first, are hopeful, show good sportsmanship, and always give your best effort. You have a choice regarding how you interpret sporting situations—choose to see the glass "half full" and assume you have control of your situation.

APPLICATION—Expect Good Things to Happen

Suggested Prayer: "Lord Jesus, help me to be happy and full of peace as I believe in you. I want to overflow with hope through the power of the Holy Spirit. I ask you to help me to see the glass 'half full' and to expect good things to happen no matter what situations I may encounter. Help me to be proactive with my actions and let my mind be aware of the things I can control. Finally, help me to except outcomes that are beyond my control. In your holy name I pray, Amen."

Take a couple of minutes to reflect on the following fictitious basketball player's mentality who chooses to see the glass "half full." When Joe Freethrow has made many free-throws in a row, he looks forward to the next free-throw because he feels "hot." Interestingly, when he has missed several free-throws in a row, he looks forward to the next free-throw because he feels that he is "due" to make the next one. Some might argue that Joe can't have it both ways because it does not make logical sense. In your notebook, write this down, "Christ wants me to believe in an <u>extraordinary</u> way!" Consider what Jesus once told his disciples:

> "...Have faith in God. I assure you that you can say to this mountain, 'May God lift you up and throw you into the sea,' and your command will be obeyed. All that's required is that you really believe and do not doubt in your heart."
> Mark 11:22-23

It is evident that Christ does not always want you to think logically—he wants you to think extraordinarily! Make it an objective to think in a more "situationally favorable" way. If you are lacking confidence, it is probable that you are struggling to see the glass "half full" and are lacking faith in your ability to control the situation. If you find that you are consistently being negative during game situations, write down in your notebook the types of situations that are causing you to be pessimistic. Assess which factors are controllable and which factors are not. Know that confident individuals consistently focus on what they can control and ignore the factors beyond their control. Expecting good things to happen and understanding what you can control will not always be easy. Use the suggested prayer frequently, and with time, answers will come. Remember, you have a choice in how you interpret sporting situations. Make the choice to assume an <u>internal locus of control</u> and see the glass "<u>half full</u>"! In the long run, this will help you with your confidence, and ultimately your performance.

SECTION I: BUILDING SELF-CONFIDENCE

Lesson 5—MODELING

"...Christ, who suffered for you, is your example. Follow in his steps." 1 Peter 2:21

We should all want to be more like Jesus Christ. If we were all simultaneously a little more like Christ for a minute, what a wonderful world we would be living in at that moment! People would think of others before themselves. People would be more humble and giving. Accomplishing <u>God's will</u> would be our primary objective. How neat that moment would be. Although none of us can ever be as great as Christ, we can all do our best to be a little more like him. Christ is our perfect example, and we should do our best to follow in his steps.

It would be neat if Jesus had a history as an athlete that was talked about in the Bible so we could always use him as a model to emulate. Imagine if we could watch a video on how Jesus would throw a football or swing a baseball bat. Surely his form would be perfect and we would have the perfect model to help teach us that particular skill. In sport psychology literature, observing the actions of someone else and then attempting to repeat the movements is called *modeling*.[9] Modeling has been shown to help with confidence because the more you watch an effective model perform a task, the more you will pay attention to the important characteristics of their movement, which over time, will help you get better at the task. And remember, the better you perform, the more confident you will be.

Unfortunately, we can't watch Jesus perform athletic skills, but we can choose models that can help us build confidence. In addition to learning skills, modeling can also help us to understand how to behave when our confidence is suffering. A champion does not hang his or her head when they are not performing well. Remember this, feelings influence behavior and behavior influences feelings.[10] The more you choose to behave like a champion, even when you are down, the better chance you have that feelings of confidence will come back. Don't forget, a champion never gives up and keeps fighting until the end. Choose to model the behaviors of champions!

APPLICATION—Modeling

Suggested prayer: "Lord Jesus, you are my perfect example, I want to follow in your steps. In regard to my sport, help me to choose role models that you approve of. Help me to behave in a way that is characteristic of a champion in your eyes. Amen."

How does a champion act on and off the playing field? What good is it if you are a champion on the court and then lose in life off the court? If you choose to be a soldier of Christ, you will always be a champion in Jesus' eyes—this is infinitely more important than winning a championship such as the Super Bowl or World Series. Know this, being a soldier of Christ will not be easy, but it will be the most rewarding experience you will ever have. Take some time to reflect on what a soldier of Christ is from the perspective of the Apostle Paul:

> **"Endure suffering along with me, as a good soldier of Christ Jesus. And as Christ's soldier, do not let yourself become tied up in the affairs of this life, for then you cannot satisfy the one who has enlisted you in his army. Follow the Lord's rules for doing his work, just as an athlete either follows the rules or is disqualified and wins no prize. Hardworking farmers are the first to enjoy the fruit of their labor. Think about what I am saying. The Lord will give you understanding in all these things." 2 Timothy 2:3-7**

Before choosing your role models, consider the characteristics of a soldier of Christ. A good role model is one that perseveres in the midst of adversity. A good role model is not caught up with how much money he or she makes, but rather is more concerned with following the rules of the Lord. Who is the hardest working athlete that you know or have heard of? Who refuses to hang their head and shoulders even when they are losing? Consider these questions before deciding who to model your game after. The next time you watch the NBA championship, or the Super Bowl, or the Stanley Cup, or some other championship game, notice which athletes thank the Lord after the game. Read the suggested prayer again and then start a list of athletes in your notebook that you will try to be like. If you find yourself in a situation in which your confidence is suffering, choose someone from your list and start acting like them. Remember, your behavior can affect how you feel. The more you act like a champion, the more you will believe in yourself!

Lesson 6—ANXIETY CAN HELP PERFORMANCE

"...The lord is my helper, so I will not be afraid..." Hebrews 13:6

It is important to understand that every athlete gets nervous before big games. If your heart is truly in the sport in which you participate, then you will likely experience "butterflies" prior to every important performance. "Butterflies" are those tingling feelings that occur in the stomach area before performing. A small percentage of individuals get so nervous that they even get sick. Many athletes do not like the feelings of butterflies and interpret them as signifying that something is wrong. The interpretation of your physical symptoms is called *somatic anxiety.*[11] Somatic anxiety can either help, hurt, or not influence your performance at all, depending on your interpretation of the symptoms. An athlete who constantly experiences a high degree of somatic anxiety and interprets their feelings negatively, will never be as confident as the athlete who understands the potential positive side of nervous feelings.

It is essential that you learn to conceptualize stomach butterflies as a natural part of sports that can actually help performance because they prime your mind and body for action. If you try to get rid of them, you will likely prevent the butterflies from helping you. Moreover, if you dwell on them, this could distract your attention away from being focused on what you need to do in order to perform successfully. An even greater potential problem is if your butterflies lead to fear. Fear can be detrimental to performance because fear prevents you from relaxing. Performing in a relaxed state is associated with peak performance. A primary factor that will determine whether fear manifests is how you interpret your feelings. A common creed in the realm of sport psychology is to not try and get rid of stomach butterflies, but rather to, try and make them "<u>fly in formation</u>."[12] Remember, some nervousness can be a good thing. If you have prepared yourself appropriately, know that you are ready. Think of butterflies as a signal from above that it is time to dance! Remember **Hebrews 13:6** and let your natural abilities take over. Once you begin performing, the butterflies will soon disappear.

APPLICATION—Anxiety Can Help Performance

Suggested Prayer: "Lord Jesus, you are my strength, my shield, and my savior. If I feel nervous or even fearful, please remind me to lean on you. I understand that I have a choice in how I interpret feelings of anxiety. Help me to believe that "butterflies" can actually help my performance. Help me to dance in the face of adversity. Amen."

Take a moment to reflect on the last time you were nervous before an important performance. What did you do to help calm yourself down? If you can remember, write it down in your notebook. Now, think about the reasons in general that cause you to feel nervous before any type of competition. Do you fear embarrassing yourself in front of your parents or friends? Do you think people will not like you if you do not do well? What are your reasons to be afraid? Sometimes it is difficult to understand why we fear failure. The fact of the matter is, no one likes to fail, and most everyone fears failure to some degree. However, it is important to understand that because you are a Christian, you really have nothing to be afraid of. Christ will always be with you! He will be with you when you win and he will be with you when you lose. No matter what the outcome of your performance is, he will love you just the same. In your notebook, write down the following quote from scripture:

> **"The LORD is my light and my salvation—so why should I be afraid? The LORD protects me from danger—so why should I tremble? When evil people come to destroy me, when my enemies and foes attack me, they will stumble and fall. Though a mighty army surrounds me, my heart will know no fear. Even if they attack me, I remain confident."**
> **Psalm 27 1:3**

Whenever you feel nervous in the future, keep **Psalm 27 1:3** in mind. Now, skip a space in your notebook and add the following sentence, *"In fact, I know that feelings of nervousness can actually help my performance because 'butterflies' get my mind and body ready for action!"* Although it will take time, if you learn to trust in the statements that you were instructed to write down, you will slowly become more and more confident before important competitions. The next time you get nervous before an important competition, remind yourself to make the butterflies "fly in formation" and play like there is no tomorrow!

REVIEW OF MAIN POINTS

1. (From the Introduction) Always keep God first and treat others as you want to be treated!

> "…You must love the Lord your God with all your heart, all your soul, and all your mind.' This is the first and greatest commandment. A second is equally important: 'Love your neighbor as yourself.' All the other commandments and all the demands of the prophets are based on these two commandments." Matthew 22:37-40

2. Practice like you play, and play like you practice!

> "Work hard so God can approve you. Be a good worker, one who does not need to be ashamed and who correctly explains the word of truth." 2 Timothy 2:15

> "Remember that in a race everyone runs, but only one person gets the prize. You also must run in such a way that you will win." 1 Corinthians 9:24

3. Use <u>positive self-talk</u>. If you are not playing well, choose to: 1. assess your performance <u>descriptively</u>, 2. make a mental-note of what you did wrong, 3. avoid being <u>judgmental</u>!

> "…I can do everything with the help of Christ who gives me the strength I need." Philippians 4:13

4. Use mental imagery. See and feel yourself performing your sport successfully.

> "…Fix your thoughts on what is true and honorable and right. Think about things that are pure and lovely and

> **admirable. Think about things that are excellent and worthy of praise." Philippians 4:8**

5. "See the glass half full!" Believe that the breaks of your sport are going to go your way.

> **"So I pray that God, who gives you hope, will keep you happy and full of peace as you believe in him. May you overflow with hope through the power of the Holy Spirit." Romans 15:13**

6. Assume an internal locus of control. Know that your actions can affect the outcome of your performance in a positive way.

> **"Dear brothers and sisters, what's the use of saying you have faith if you don't prove it by your actions?" James 2:14**

7. Keep your head held high when feeling down—behavior influences feelings! Choose "soldiers of Christ" to model your game after.

> **"...Christ, who suffered for you, is your example. Follow in his steps." 1 Peter 2:21**

8. "Stomach butterflies" can help your performance. Don't try and get rid of them, get them to "<u>fly in formation</u>."

> **"...The lord is my helper, so I will not be afraid..." Hebrews 13:6**

REFERENCES: Building Self-Confidence

1. Weinberg, R.S., & Gould, D. (1999). *Foundations of Sport and Exercise Psychology* (2nd ed.). Champaign, IL: Human Kinetics.

2. Barnett, G., & Gregorian, V. (1996). *High Hopes.* New York: Warner Books.

3. Williams, J.M. (2001). *Applied Sport Psychology: Personal Growth to Peak Performance,* 4th ed.. Mountain View, CA: Mayfield Publishing.

4. Gallwey, W.T. (1999). *The Inner Game of Work.* New York: Random House.

5. Orlick, T. (1990). *In Pursuit of Excellence.* Champaign, IL: Leisure Press.

6. Martin, K.A., Moritz, S.E., & Hall, C.R. (1999). Imagery use in sport: A literature review and applied model. *The Sport Psychologist,* 13, 245-268.

7. Vealy, R.S. (2001). Understanding and enhancing self-confidence in athletes. In R.N. Singer, H.A. Hausenblas, & C.M. Janelle (Eds.), *Handbook of Sport Psychology,* 2nd ed. (pp. 550-565). New York: John Wiley & Sons.

8. Singer, R.N. (1984). *Sustaining Motivation in sport.* Tallahassee, FL: Sport Consultants International, Inc.

9. McCullagh, P. & Weiss, M.R. (2001). Modeling: Considerations for motor skill performance and psychological responses. In R.N.

Singer, H.A. Hausenblas, & C.M. Janelle (Eds.), *Handbook of Sport Psychology*, 2nd ed. (pp. 205-238). New York: John Wiley & Sons.

10. Lazarus, R.S. (1991). Cognition and motivation in emotion. *American Psychologist*, 46, 352-367.

11. Martens, R., Vealey, R.S., & Burton, D. (1990) *Competitive anxiety in sport*. Champaign, IL: Human Kinetics.

12. Hanton, S., & Jones, G. (1999). The acquisition and development of cognitive skills and strategies: I. Making the butterflies fly in formation. *The Sport Psychologist*, 13, 1-21.

SECTION II: PURPOSE, MOTIVATION, ATTITUDE, AND GOALS

"Look here, you people who say, 'Today or tomorrow we are going to a certain town and will stay there a year. We will do business there and make a profit.' How do you know what will happen tomorrow? For your life is like the morning fog—it's here a little while, then it's gone. What you ought to say is, 'If the Lord wants us to, we will live and do this or that.' Otherwise you will be boasting about your own plans, and all such boasting is evil." James 4:13-16

In the previous section, the importance of self-confidence was discussed and several techniques to improve your "building" were explained. However, it is important to emphasize that your self-confidence should always be acceptable to God. There are many athletes in amateur and professional sports who are confident and successful but who do not put God first in their lives. What good is it to be confident and successful in one's own opinion or from the perspective of others if Jesus Christ himself is not happy with the way you express your confidence? Keep in mind that although confidence is associated with peak performance, displaying too much confidence is <u>not</u> a good thing—never let your confidence turn into arrogance.

Your attitude will influence how your confidence is expressed, so it is important that you work on developing an attitude that is pleasing to God. To do this, you will need to be committed to a Christian path. Your purpose as an athlete, your motives, your attitude, and the goals you set will all influence each other and each is an essential ingredient for you to reach your potential. In this section, these topics are discussed systematically with the goal of helping you develop an approach to sports that is pleasing to Christ. Remember, society's definition of success is not always the same as the way Jesus defines it. It will take time to understand precisely what success means from a Christian standpoint, but with persistent prayer and patience, answers will be forthcoming. As you read the next several pages, keep in mind that what Jesus wants for you is bigger than any accomplishment you are capable of dreaming!

Lesson 1—PURPOSE—WHY DO YOU PLAY?

"Keep on asking, and you will be given what you ask for. Keep on looking, and you will find. Keep on knocking, and the door will be opened. For everyone who asks, receives. Everyone who seeks, finds. And the door is opened to everyone who knocks." Matthew 7:7-8

Different people play sports for different reasons. Some people play for the enjoyment they feel while performing, while others participate because their friends are involved or to keep their bodies fit. A very small percentage of people play sports professionally in order to make a living. For some individuals, determining the role that sports will have in their lives will be easy, but for many, it may be difficult. No matter what role sports will ultimately play in your life, know that as a Christian, you should be motivated to bring glory to God in some way. That is, when you are successful, give the credit to Jesus.

If you are not sure how sports will affect the direction of your life, it is important to consult with your personal coach and biggest fan, Jesus Christ. It is not uncommon for athletes to question why they play sports, particularly when things are not going well. Uncertainty will always be part of sports to some degree, and answers will often be difficult to find. Athletes often have big egos and attempt to find the answers on their own, without any help. You may be able to make sense of things from time to time on your own, but we all need help during some points in our lives.

Parents, coaches, and friends are good sources of information and should be involved with your decision-making processes, but it is best to go to Jesus first, because he knows the best plan for you! In **Psalm 32:8** the Lord says, **"...I will guide you along the best**

pathway for your life. I will advise you and watch over you."
Keep in mind that answers regarding your path will not always come immediately, but they will come if you are humbly persistent with prayer. Make it a priority to always consult with Jesus first about the direction of your life and then live with a burning desire to be the best you can be. Remember, you have the chance to bring glory to God in whatever you choose to do with sports and in life. Make the best of your opportunity!

Helpful Scripture: "Show me the path where I should walk, O LORD; point out the right road for me to follow. Lead me by your truth and teach me, for you are the God who saves me. All day long I put my hope in you." Psalm 25:4-5

Lesson 2—MOTIVATION

"So be careful not to jump to conclusions before the Lord returns as to whether or not someone is faithful. When the Lord comes, he will bring our deepest secrets to light and will reveal our private motives. And then God will give to everyone whatever praise is due." 1 Corinthians 4:5

No matter what role your sport currently plays or will play in your life, it is important that your motives for participating are acceptable to God. *Motivation* concerns the factors related to why an individual starts and persists at some activity. As you seek to understand the right path for you, assess what motivates you in terms of intrinsic and extrinsic motivation. *Intrinsic motivation* means being motivated to do something because it is inherently rewarding (e.g., fun, challenging, etc.), while *extrinsic motivation* means being motivated to do something for the purpose of some external result (e.g., winning, earning money, rewards, etc.).[1] Intrinsic motivation is an end in itself and extrinsic motivation serves as a means to an end.

Understand that if you want to be the best athlete you can be, a balance of intrinsic and extrinsic motivation is necessary. If you only have extrinsic motivation, such as earning awards or fame, sports may become more tedious than rewarding, and you may eventually burnout and quit altogether. If you only have intrinsic motivation, such as having fun, then you might not push yourself when the going gets tough. Understanding precisely what motivates you may take some time—keep asking Jesus and your motives will eventually become clearer. Above all else, you want your motives to be acceptable to Christ.

In your notebook, make a list of all the reasons you can think of that concern your motivation to play sports. If you can, try to list the reasons in order of importance. When you finish, reflect on what motivates you. For now, your motives may be somewhat hazy. Hopefully, by the end of this book, you will have intrinsic and extrinsic motives that are acceptable to Christ. For this to occur, you will need to have the right attitude, which will be discussed in the pages that follow.

Suggested prayer: "Lord Jesus, help me to understand what motivates me to play sports. I want my motives to be acceptable to you. In your holy name I pray, Amen."

ATTITUDE (Lessons 3-6)

"Love is patient and kind. Love is not jealous or boastful or proud or rude. Love does not demand its own way. Love is not irritable, and it keeps no record of when it has been wronged. It is never glad about injustice but rejoices whenever the truth wins out. Love never gives up, never loses faith, is always hopeful, and endures through every circumstance." 1 Corinthians 13:4-7

Attitudes are relatively stable evaluations of persons, objects, or situations.[2] Although attitudes tend to be consistent, they can be changed, and sometimes need to be. If a coach is having a problem with a particular athlete, the player may be told that he or she needs an "attitude adjustment." Players who hear this often do not understand what is meant by an attitude adjustment and coaches sometimes do not do a very good job of explaining what they mean.

Athletes need coaching and guidance that is specific, and simply telling an athlete that they need an attitude adjustment will likely cause the player to become defensive, and perhaps unteachable. If an athlete is perceived as having a bad attitude, it is very likely that the player is not letting love dictate their attitude and actions. For the rest of your life, you have the choice to have a good attitude or a bad one both on and off the playing field. If you commit to playing with love in your heart, then it is safe to assume you will have an attitude that will be admired by those you encounter.

Love is a mystery and is not talked about very much in the realm of science, although the majority of people in the world believe in love in some way. Only God knows how to define love precisely, but in **1 Corinthians,** Apostle Paul does give us an idea about what love is and what love is not. In the next several lessons of Section II, love, as it is described in **1 Corinthians 13:4-7**, will be discussed in the context of sports and attitude. As you read, consider this question, "*Are you currently playing your sport with an attitude influenced by love?*" The sooner you make the commitment to letting love dictate your attitude and actions, the sooner your potential as a Christian athlete can be realized!

Lesson 3: ATTITUDE—PATIENCE AND SPORTSMANSHIP

"Love is patient and kind…" 1 Corinthians 13:4

Without patience, your potential as an athlete will be limited. It is safe to say that all champion athletes have had to exercise patience at some point in their athletic careers. Patience is such an important skill that it will be discussed again in Section III in the context of adversity. For now, consider the importance of patience as it relates to sportsmanship. The ability to display good sportsmanship will be difficult if not impossible, without some appreciation of patience. You can almost guarantee that a player who refuses to shake hands with the opposing team after losing a game is self-focused and lacks patience in him or herself.

The outcome of your particular sport will not always go your way. When it doesn't, it is important to be patient and respectful—it is not all about you! It goes without saying that good sportsmanship should be a primary objective for a Christian athlete. Therefore, patience and kindness go hand in hand. Know that being kind does not mean being soft, but rather, it means showing positive emotions for others. Always offer respect to your opponents before, during, and after the game. Look them in the eye and let them know that you appreciate their competition. However, when you play be fierce and play with desire and passion.

> **"Remember that in a race everyone runs, but only one person gets the prize. You also must run in such a way that you will win." 1 Corinthians 9:24**

Mike Singletary, a Christian Hall of Fame linebacker, always played to win the prize. He is considered one of the most intense and fierce football players to ever play the game. Mike was a member of the Super Bowl XX champion Chicago Bears and was the NFL Defensive Player of the Year three times. He put many hard hits on his opponents, but always made it a point to offer respect to his fellow competitors. As a result, he is respected as both a great player and a great Christian man. In the NFL, a good hit is part of the game. But remember, it is just a game, and the way it is played should be dictated by love.

Suggested Prayer: "Lord Jesus, please grant me patience as I play my sport. Help me to be kind to others as I play with passion and intensity. Amen."

SECTION II: PURPOSE, MOTIVATION, ATTITUDE, AND GOALS

Lesson 4—ATTITUDE AND WHAT LOVE IS NOT

"...Love is not jealous or boastful or proud or rude. Love does not demand its own way..." 1 Corinthians 13:4-5

If you find jealously in your heart, then you lack love. "**Do not covet...**" what others have is one of the Ten Commandments (**Exodus 20:17**). We have all experienced jealousy at some point in our lives. However, you should try to be happy for others and for what they have. Love is also <u>not about being boastful</u>. Today, there are many athletes who are not afraid to tell people how great they are. It is not uncommon for professional athletes to complain that they should be making more money because they are better than "so and so." It is less common to hear a professional athlete talk about how blessed he or she is for just getting the opportunity to play sports for a living. As was discussed in Section I, you should attempt to model Christ. Never forget that Christ himself was not boastful even though he saved mankind!

> "**Your attitude should be the same that Christ Jesus had. Though he was God, he did not demand and cling to his rights as God. He made himself nothing; he took the humble position of a slave and appeared in human form. And in human form he obediently humbled himself even further by dying a criminal's death on a cross.**" **Philippians 2:5-8.**

So when considering your deeds, know that Jesus enjoys watching a thankful person more than one who brags about his or her accomplishments. Moreover, **"God sets himself against the proud, but he shows favor to the humble" James 4:6**. Fortunately, there are many athletes in this world who are both thankful and humble. However, we need many more. It is your duty as a Christian athlete to do everything you can to be one of them.

Suggested Prayer: "Lord Jesus, thank you for all of your blessings. You have given me so much. Help me to be happy for what others have and not to be jealous. Let my disposition be humble as I seek your will. Amen."

SECTION II: PURPOSE, MOTIVATION, ATTITUDE, AND GOALS

Lesson 5—ATTITUDE AND FORGIVENESS

"...Love is not irritable, and it keeps no record of when it has been wronged. It is never glad about injustice but rejoices whenever the truth wins out." 1 Corinthians 13:5-6

We all get irritable from time to time. When circumstances don't go our way it can be frustrating. Moreover, if we feel that we have been treated unfairly, whether intentionally or not, our emotions can affect our behavior in a negative way. A simple example is when a referee makes a bad call during a game. No one likes it when a bad call is made. However, some players and coaches react more intensely than others. In basketball, if a player or coach jumps in a referee's face, then a technical foul may result. It is obvious that the ability to control one's emotional reactions to bad calls or other upsetting situations is an important attribute of a successful athlete. What is less evident, but even more important, is how an individual thinks and acts when the game continues.

Remember, love "<u>keeps no record of when it has been wronged</u>." Therefore, if you hold grudges or can't "get over it" when you feel you've been wronged, then you are allowing yourself to get away from the power of love. Coaches, parents, referees, friends, foes, all make mistakes. In order to play with love in your heart, you must develop the ability to forgive and move on. <u>Life isn't always fair, but justice will win out</u>! God is the ultimate judge and we will all be judged according to our motives and actions. Jesus teaches us about judging others in **Matthew 7:1-2**:

> "Stop judging others, and you will not be judged. For others will treat you as you treat them. Whatever measure you

use in judging others, it will be used to measure how you are judged."

It is not your duty as a Christian athlete to judge, it is your duty to forgive and believe that justice will ultimately be served. The ability to forgive will not always be easy, but it is a skill and like any other skill, it needs to be practiced. The sooner you learn to forgive and let things go, the better you will be at focusing on the things that you need to do in order to be successful.

Suggested Prayer: "Lord Jesus, help me to be effective at controlling my emotions. If I am wronged in any way, help me not to hold grudges or judge others, but rather to have a forgiving heart. Amen."

Lesson 6—ATTITUDE AND ENDURANCE

"Love never gives up, never loses faith, is always hopeful, and endures through every circumstance." 1 Corinthians 13:7

The power of love is awesome—love is the ultimate gift from God! Imagine for a minute Jesus Christ watching the World Series, the Super Bowl, or some other major sporting event. Who do you think he roots for? Do you think he pulls for the team with the most Christians? Does he show favor to the underdog or the home team? Would he intervene to ensure that his team wins? Which would Jesus prefer, that you focus all of your attention on winning or all of your attention on playing with love? No one but Jesus himself knows for sure the answers to these questions, but it would be a safe bet that if you play with love in your heart, you will win in Jesus' eyes. Isn't this the most important kind of winning?

As previously mentioned, success for the Christian athlete needs to be defined differently than just winning the game. Imagine for a minute yourself as an athlete who never gives up, never loses faith, is always hopeful, and endures through every circumstance. Wow! Can you see how good you can be? The sky is the limit! Now focus on the last part of the sentence, "endures through every circumstance." Some might interpret this as winning, as in scoring more points than your opponent, no matter what the situation. But <u>to endure is different than to win on the scoreboard</u>. It is much more difficult to jump back on your horse when you get kicked off than when you beat all the other horses in a race! The athlete who endures always keeps fighting even after a defeat. The athlete who endures keeps his or her head up when he or she fails. The athlete who endures is the one that is hopeful, faithful, and never gives up! As you continue to consider and possibly change what success means to you, be sure to include the term "endure" somewhere, and give every effort you have to win in God's eyes.

Suggested Prayer: "Lord Jesus, help me to be a person that doesn't give up. Help me to strive to be more hopeful and faithful as I play my sport and live my life. Help me to endure the difficulties that I may encounter and be with me as I give my best today. Amen."

SECTION II: PURPOSE, MOTIVATION, ATTITUDE, AND GOALS

Lesson 7—GOAL-SETTING PHILOSOPHY

"When I think of the wisdom and scope of God's plan, I fall to my knees and pray to the Father, the Creator of everything in heaven and earth." Ephesians 3:14-15

Great athletes set goals and work hard to achieve them. ***Goal-setting*** involves establishing objectives that relate to some level of proficiency for a given pursuit.[3] It is important to understand that in order to reach your potential, you will need to set goals. Moreover, it is important to set goals that God approves. Don't forget that Christ has a grand plan for you and you should **"[b]e glad for all God is planning for you..." Romans 12:12.** Remember, what God ultimately wants for us is bigger than we can currently comprehend.

> **"Now glory be to God! By his mighty power at work within us, he is able to accomplish infinitely more than we would ever dare to ask or hope." Ephesians 3:20**

So goal-setting for the Christian athlete is somewhat of a paradox. It is important to set goals, even though the ultimate goal according to God's plan is not always clear. Goal-setting will not always be easy, so it is important that you keep your philosophy of goal-setting simple.

"Let love be your highest goal..." 1 Corinthians 14:1. As you begin your goal-setting process, refer back to the lessons on *attitude* and strive to play with an attitude characterized by love. Next, understand that God has a long-term plan for you that is bigger than you can currently comprehend. Therefore, do not attempt to map-out your whole career, because you want Christ to be in control of your life, not you! Keep an open mind and understand that making adjustments to your goals is characteristic of a Christian mindset. Finally, stay close to God when making your goals. "**Draw close to God, and God will draw close to you…**" **James 4:8.** That is, ask Jesus what you should focus your attention and effort on and have faith that the Holy Spirit will guide you down the path God wants you to follow.

APPLICATION—Goal-Setting Philosophy

Suggested Prayer: "Lord Jesus, help me to set goals that that will ultimately help bring glory to you. I understand that you have a plan for me that is bigger than I can currently comprehend. Let the goals that I set be touched by the grace of the Holy Spirit so that my path may be in line with your will. Amen."

Take a few minutes to <u>write down</u> in your notebook all the goals you can think of that you would like to accomplish as an athlete. Goals are only dreams, until they are <u>written down</u>.

Write down whatever goals come to mind. Once you are finished, take some time to reflect on what you have written. Think of your goals as they pertain to your life as a Christian athlete. Which of your goals do you think would be acceptable to God? Ideally, the primary goal for a Christian athlete should be to bring glory to Christ in some way! However, most of us are primarily focused on ourselves so it is unusual to see this listed as a goal. For many Christians, bringing glory to God doesn't become a burning passion until after some time has passed. Know that the sooner Jesus becomes an integral part of your plan, the quicker you will be on the path to a fulfilling life. Keep your eye on the ultimate prize, which is life through Jesus!

> "...And let us run with endurance the race that God has set before us. We do this by keeping our eyes on Jesus, on whom our faith depends from start to finish." Hebrews 12:1-2

Bringing glory to God can be done in many ways. After winning Super Bowl XXIV, MVP Kurt Warner, former quarterback for the Los Angeles Rams, made it a point to publicly thank Jesus first before talking about what happened during the game. Kurt gave the glory of the victory to Christ! When David Robinson, two-time NBA champion and league MVP in 1995, retired from the NBA, he publicly thanked Jesus in a memorable retirement celebration. Although these two men did accomplish a lot, you don't have to be an NFL or NBA MVP to bring glory to Christ. If your goals include winning, and you plan to give Jesus the credit for your success, then the goals you set and achieve can help give you the opportunity to bring glory to him. Take some time to look back at the goals you wrote down. If you are not sure if your goals would be acceptable to Jesus, then ask him to help you with your list! Continued use of the *suggested prayer* may help you find peace with your goals and direction.

Lesson 8—GOAL-SETTING PROCESS

"No, dear friends, I am still not all I should be, but I am focusing all my energies on this one thing: Forgetting the past and looking forward to what lies ahead, I strain to reach the end of the race and receive the prize for which God, through Christ Jesus, is calling us up to heaven." Philippians 3:13-14

In the above scripture, the Apostle Paul's comments to the Philippians relate to the importance of this simple creed—**learn** from the past, **plan** for the future, and **live** in the present. Goal-setting will help you plan for the future. Before developing your plan, it is important to discuss a few goal-setting principles which have been shown to be beneficial.[4] First, set only a few goals! Athletes who set too many goals limit their potential because quality time and effort gets dispersed among too many different areas. Focus on a few specific goals that are challenging, but realistic and attainable. For example, if you are a miler and your best mile is currently seven minutes, a realistic but difficult goal would be to run a 6:45 mile by the end of the month. Being specific helps you to focus on precisely what you want to accomplish. If the goals are too general (e.g., to get faster at the mile) or too easy, then they will not be of much value because they will not push you to be your best. However, if they are too difficult and not ultimately attainable, then frustration may result which can cause you to lose confidence. Knowing whether you are being realistic or not may be difficult at first, but it will get easier the more you learn about yourself.

Goal-setting is a process. You will need to make adjustments to your goals and your goal-setting techniques as you progress through the years. The setting of short-term and long-term goals is an integral part of the process. Long-term goals, such as bringing glory to Christ or winning a championship, serve primarily as ongoing motivation. It is essential that you have long-term goals because they will dictate the direction of your path and will help you persevere when the going gets tough. However, the accomplishment of many short-term goals is needed before your ultimate goals will be realized. Think of your long-term goals as being at the top of a staircase and your short-term goals as the steps that will get you there. You may trip and fall on one of the steps and have to take a step back before taking several forward. As long as you keep your "eye on the prize" and keep making adjustments where needed, you will find a way to get to the top!

Helpful Scripture: "So I run straight to the goal with purpose in every step." 1 Corinthians 9:26

APPLICATION—Goal-Setting Process

Suggested Prayer: "Lord Jesus, help me to learn from my mistakes, plan for the future, and live in the present. Please guide me as I seek to make and achieve goals that you will approve. Amen."

You will need to designate a place to record and monitor you goal-setting process. A good idea is to get a daily planner and a calendar that you can devote to keeping track of your short and long-term goals. In regard to your goals for the year, go through the calendar and write down on a specific date the specific goals that you would like to accomplish. If you can, get a large bulletin board and pin the months of the calendar next to each other so that you can see at least 6 months at one time (12 months is even better).

It is a good idea to have a good balance of <u>outcome</u> and <u>performance</u> goals. ***Outcome goals*** concern the result between opponents, such as winning a 1st place medal or a team championship; whereas ***performance goals*** represent personal improvement (e.g., improving from a 7 minute mile to a 6:45 mile).[5] Both outcome and performance goals are important, but know that performance goals are more controllable. If find that you are not meeting your outcome goals, focus on your performance goals and understand that you should be proud of any kind of personal improvement that you achieve. Before each week starts, look at your calendar and see what goals are coming up. Know that the purpose of outcome and performance goals is to provide you with motivation to get better. However, it is important to understand that <u>during</u> a particular practice or game, you should shift your focus from <u>performance</u> and <u>outcome</u> goals, to <u>process goals.</u>

Process goals are objectives that relate specifically to doing your best during a particular performance.[6] For example, keeping your head down when swinging a baseball bat, or focusing on staying relaxed during a long run. There are many process goals that are imperative for success in each sport and it is important that you consult with your coaches to understand which process goals are more important than others. If you focus too much on outcome and performance goals during a particular competition, then you could potentially distract your attention away from the things you need to be focusing on (i.e., process goals) in order to do your best. More specific techniques to help you with your focus during game situations will be discussed in Section IV (Playing in the Zone). For now, write this down in your notebook, "*The achievement of process goals will lead to the achievement of performance goals which will lead to the achievement of outcome goals.*" Be blessed as you achieve one step at a time!

REVIEW OF MAIN POINTS

1. <u>Ask Jesus</u> about the purpose of sports in your life.

> "Keep on asking, and you will be given what you ask for. Keep on looking, and you will find. Keep on knocking, and the door will be opened. For everyone who asks, receives. Everyone who seeks, finds. And the door is opened to everyone who knocks." Matthew 7:7-9

2. Monitor your motives in terms of <u>intrinsic</u> and <u>extrinsic</u> reasons and consider whether they are <u>acceptable to God</u>.

> "So be careful not to jump to conclusions before the Lord returns as to whether or not someone is faithful. When the Lord comes, he will bring our deepest secrets to light and will reveal our private motives. And then God will give to everyone whatever praise is due." 1 Corinthians 4:5

3. Play your sport with an <u>attitude characterized by love</u> and "(l)et love be your highest goal…" 1 Corinthians 14:1

> "Love is patient and kind. Love is not jealous or boastful or proud or rude. Love does not demand its own way. Love is not irritable, and it keeps no record of when it has been wronged. It is never glad about injustice but rejoices whenever the truth wins out. Love never gives up, never loses faith, is always hopeful, and endures through every circumstance." 1 Corinthians 13:4-7

4. Seek <u>God's plan for you</u>, which is <u>bigger</u> than you can currently comprehend.

> "Now glory be to God! By his mighty power at work within us, he is able to accomplish infinitely more than we would ever dare to ask or hope." Ephesians 3:20-21

5. Keep Jesus in mind during the goal-setting process and make it your goal to bring <u>glory to Christ</u> in some way!

> "...And let us run with endurance the race that God has set before us. We do this by keeping our eyes on Jesus, on whom our faith depends from start to finish." Hebrews 12:1-2

6. Make *specific* <u>outcome</u>, <u>performance</u>, and <u>process</u> goals. Remember, process goals lead to performance goals, which lead to outcome goals.

> "So I run straight to the goal with purpose in every step." 1 Corinthians 9:26

REFERENCES: Direction, Motivation, Attitude, and Goals

1. Vallerand, R.J., & Rousseau, F.L. (2001). Intrinsic and extrinsic motivation in sport and exercise: A review using the hierarchical model of intrinsic and extrinsic motivation. In R.N. Singer, H.A. Hausenblas, & C.M. Janelle (Eds.), *Handbook of Sport Psychology*, 2nd ed. (pp. 389-416). New York: John Wiley & Sons.

2. Wood, S.E., & Wood, E.R.G (2002). *The World of Psychology* (4th ed.). Boston, MA: Allyn & Bacon.

3. Weinberg, R.S., Gould, D. (1999). *Foundations of Sport and Exercise Psychology* (2nd ed.). Champaign, IL: Human Kinetics.

4. Gould, D. (2001). Goal setting for peak performance. In J.M. Williams (Ed.), *Applied Sport Psychology: Personal Growth to Peak Performance,* 4th ed. (pp.190-205). Mountain View, CA: Mayfield Publishing.

5. Burton, D., Naylor, S., & Holliday, B. (2001). Goal setting in sport: Investigating the goal effectiveness paradox. In R.N. Singer, H.A. Hausenblas, & C.M. Janelle (Eds.), *Handbook of Sport Psychology*, 2nd ed. (pp. 497-528). New York: John Wiley & Sons.

6. Hardy, L., Jones, G., & Gould, D. (1996). *Understanding Psychological Preparation for Sport: Theory and Practice of Elite Performers.* Chichester, UK: Wiley.

SECTION III: DEALING WITH ADVERSITY

"God is our refuge and strength, always ready to help in times of trouble." Psalm 46:1

We will all face adversity in life. Each of us has a choice regarding how we deal with the troubles that come our way. Some people will feel more stress than others. Some will ignore their problems and choose not to deal with them. It is important to understand that to be a successful athlete, you must learn to deal effectively with adversity. Remember, how you deal with adversity is a choice! Know that Christ is ready to help you with your troubles, but before he will intercede, you must first call on his name. It is written that **"[t]he LORD hears his people when they call to him for help..." Psalm 34:17.** This section will help you deal with adversity by leaning on Jesus.

> **"He will shield you with his wings. He will shelter you with feathers. His faithful promises are your armor and protection." Psalm 91:4**

A mindset focused on the promises of Jesus Christ will instill an underlying belief in your ability to persevere through the trying times that you will face as an athlete. As a soldier of Christ, your armor will be the skills you learn from the principles in the Bible. Adversity may come your way in different forms, such as negative peer pressure, criticism, slumping, and/or injuries, to name a few. At times, adversity may appear in unexpected ways not discussed in this book. If you are mentally equipped to cope with adversities before they arise, they will ultimately be easier to overcome. Patience and prayer are essential ingredients to your mental-game and ways to improve these skills are emphasized is this section. Remember, Christ is ready to help you. Call on his name and receive the comfort, protection, and strength that he wants you to have.

Lesson 1—ADVERSITY IS PART OF THE GAME

"Dear friends, don't be surprised at the fiery trials you are going through, as if something strange were happening to you. Instead, be very glad—because these trials will make you partners with Christ in his suffering, and afterward you will have the wonderful joy of sharing his glory when it is displayed to all the world." 1 Peter 4:12-13

As in life, adversity will always be part of sports. In **1 Peter 4:12-13,** we are warned that some form of adversity awaits us and we need to be strong in Christ in order to get through it. There is not one successful athlete in the world that has not gone through some type of adversity during some point in their career. A famous athlete who comes to mind is Jackie Robinson of the former Brooklyn Dodgers. Jackie is credited with breaking the color barrier in major league baseball. During the 1940's, African Americans were "unofficially" prevented from playing in the major leagues. However, the Brooklyn Dodgers went against tradition and signed Jackie Robinson to play second base. Jackie eventually became a Hall of Fame player, but his path was filled with adversity. Throughout his career, he received constant racial abuse and even threats on his life. But Jackie endured the punishment because he knew he was playing for a higher cause—he was breaking the color barrier!

Jackie's experience with adversity was extreme. But don't forget Jesus, who endured the greatest adversity of all, his crucifixion. As an athlete, you will never face the adversities that Jesus had to face. But make no mistake, you will face adversity. Do not interpret preparation for adversity as being a negative concept. Instead, approach your sport with an understanding that adversity is part of the game. If you do this, you will be able to better deal with adversity when it comes. If you feel afraid in any way, remember to exercise an attitude characterized by love **"…because love expels all fear" 1 John 4:18**. So be as optimistic as you can when adversity appears in your life. Know that we all must share in suffering in some way, but in the end, we get to share in Christ's glory. Always remember that adversity is part of sports, and never forget that Jesus is always with you.

APPLICATION—Adversity is Part of the Game

Helpful Scripture: "[Lord Jesus], [t]urn to me and have mercy on me, for I am alone and in deep distress. My problems go from bad to worse. Oh, save me from them all! Feel my pain and see my trouble. Forgive all my sins. [Amen]." Psalm 26:16-18

Take a few minutes to ponder some of the troubles in your life that may affect how you play on the field. In your notebook, write down the things that bring you down. Just brainstorm and write down, or at least think about, your past, present, and potential future adversities. Problems have the potential to bring all of us down. Some people have more than others, but everyone has their share. However, successful people deal with their adversities more effectively than people who struggle just to get by. Because trouble will eventually come your way in some form, it is important that you learn to deal with adversity effectively through an optimistic mindset so that you can cope with your issues and become stronger.

> **"...[W]henever trouble comes your way, let it be an opportunity for joy. For when your faith is tested, your endurance has a chance to grow. So let it grow, for when your endurance is fully developed, you will be strong in character and ready for anything." James 1:2-4**

It has been demonstrated in sport psychology literature that athletes who have effective coping skills often perceive threatening situations as a challenge and an opportunity for growth.[1] The next time you are feeling down or threatened, remember that you have the strongest power in the world on your side, Jesus Christ! Depend on him and remember what was previously mentioned, feelings can

<u>affect thoughts and behavior</u> and <u>behavior and thoughts can affect feelings</u>.[2] When you are feeling down or even scared, don't slouch your shoulders and think negatively. Instead, handle adversity effectively by forcing yourself to start behaving like a champion! <u>Do not let your depressed feelings affect how you think and behave, but rather, make your behavior and thoughts dictate how you will feel.</u> Use the mental skills discussed in Section I. Remember modeling, keep your head up, your shoulders back, and walk like a champion. Use mental imagery and positive self-talk—fire yourself up! Remember, with adversity comes the opportunity to build strength in your character. Never let an opportunity go by!

Lesson 2—WORRY AND PRAYER

"Don't worry about anything, instead, pray about everything. Tell God what you need, and thank him for all he has done. If you do this, you will experience God's peace, which is far more wonderful than the human mind can understand..." Philippians 4:6-7

We all worry, it is a natural part of human nature. Some people worry more than others, but we all worry to some degree. When you perform your best however, worry disappears. In sport, the phenomenon of worrying about one's impending performance is called **cognitive anxiety**.[3] Like somatic anxiety (the perception of physiological symptoms discussed in Section I), a certain degree of cognitive anxiety can potentially help performance because it elicits alertness. However, the athlete who worries throughout a particular contest will nearly always do worse than the athlete who minimizes worry. In fact, peak performance is characterized by the absence of fear.[4] Therefore, it is essential that you learn to prevent worry from affecting your athletic potential.

So how do you minimize cognitive anxiety? Prayer is without a doubt the most important mental skill for a Christian athlete. Prayer puts us under God's control. You will be stronger mentally when you are dependent on Christ than if you depend on yourself alone to cure all of your worries. It is written in the Bible that Christ's **"...power works best in your weakness..." 2 Corinthians 12:9.** Therefore, it is possible to be strong even when you feel weak if you depend on Jesus! Hence, always pray before you play! Ask Christ to be with you while you perform and then surrender all of your worries to him. Understand that some worry may be inevitable during important contests. Negative thoughts might jump in and out of your mind even when you really don't want them to. But thoughts are just thoughts, and as long as you do not dwell on them, thoughts cannot do you any harm. Remember, because you believe in Jesus Christ, you have the ultimate power in the world on your side. Although he is pulling for you, you will not always win every game that you play. But more importantly, because he loves you, you will always win in life! Keep this in perspective before every competition.

APPLICATION—Worry and Prayer

Suggested Prayer: "Lord Jesus, thank you for all you have done for me. I have so many blessings. But I have a lot of worries on my mind, such as......(list your worries).......... I am going to turn my worries over to you and let you handle them. Help me to have faith in you and your plan for me. I need you more than anything in the world. Amen."

Dealing with worry through prayer is the focus of this application. Throughout this book, suggested prayers have been given. However, it is important that you develop your own style of prayer based on the guidelines set forth in the Bible. Keep the following suggestions from scripture in mind when you pray:

> 1. "Keep on asking, and you will be given what you ask for..." Mathew 7:7

Some people do not pray, because they feel guilty asking for things. Some might not pray because they fear they will make a mistake during prayer. It is important to understand, that the most important thing regarding prayer is that you pray frequently! Jesus wants to hear from you. **"And we can be confident that he will listen to us whenever we ask him for anything in line with his will" 1 John 5:14.** He knows that you are not perfect and he understands that you will make mistakes. Fortunately, he loves you anyway and will always make time for you. Don't worry, he is powerful enough to handle everyone's problems simultaneously!

> 2. "But when you ask him, be sure that you really expect him to answer, for a doubtful mind is as unsettled as a wave of the sea that is driven and tossed by the wind. People like

**this should not expect to receive anything from the Lord."
James 1:6-7**

It is important to believe that something is going to happen when you pray. God speaks to us through the Holy Spirit in different ways. It could be through dreams or feelings, or some other medium. Although prayers will not always be answered immediately, <u>if you truly believe</u>, he will answer you in some way. Remember, Christ's plan for you is not always the same as yours. As has been emphasized in this section, sometimes you will have to endure adversity. However, the more you pray and trust in Jesus, the more you will experience the peace of Christ's love. Take a few moments to tell Jesus about your troubles and your wishes. He wants to hear from you. Know in your heart that he will answer in some way.

Lesson 3—PATIENCE AND ADVERSITY

"Be glad for all God is planning for you. Be patient in trouble, and always be prayerful." Romans 12:12

As was mentioned in Section II, patience is a key virtue in life and in sport. Like prayer, patience is such an important skill that it needs to be emphasized again. Without the ability to be patient, you will have greater potential for frustration, which could limit your potential as an athlete. It is important that you commit to developing a will that is characterized by patience. If you play team sports and are not getting as much playing time as you would like, be patient—keep working hard and you will get your chance. If you are slumping and nothing seems to be going your way, be patient—things will turn around soon. If you are injured, be patient, God's power can heal your wounds with time. There are many ways that adversity will cause frustration in your life. It is during these times that your faith will be tested and patience with prayer will be needed.

An athlete who illustrates the concepts of patience and adversity is Dan Jansen, a former Olympic speed-skater for the United States of America. In 1988, Dan was favored to win both the 500 and 1000-meter speed-skating events in Calgary. Unfortunately, he learned that his sister Jane died the morning he was to perform the 500. Dan was unable to stay focused during the race and fell shortly after the start. He was eliminated from the event. Three days later he fell again during the 1000 and did not finish the race. Jansen was devastated and would have to wait until 1992 to get another shot at a gold medal. Unfortunately for Dan, he did not skate his best at the 1992 Games in Albertville and finished a disappointing 4th in the 500 and 26th in the 1000. He was forced to be patient again. Two years later, at the Olympic Games in Norway, Jansen would get another chance to win the gold medal. Unfortunately, Jansen slipped during the 500 race and finished a disappointing 8th. With one last chance in the 1000, Jansen finally won the gold in one of the most memorable events in Olympic history—he broke the world record! Without patience, Dan would have never been able to triumph over adversity the way he did.

APPLICATION—Patience and Adversity

Suggested Prayer: "Lord Jesus, grant me the patience to get through the tough situations that I face. I know that your will takes time, and I know patience will help me become stronger in character. In your holy name I pray, Amen."

Reflect for a moment on your ability to be patient during frustrating situations. Do you consider yourself a patient person? If you do not know the answer to this question, ask your coaches, friends, or family members. If they do not emphasize that you are a very patient person, then you can improve in this area. One of the primary reasons people are not good at being more patient is that they do not commit to <u>becoming</u> more patient. If you want to get better at being more patient, you must first <u>commit to getting better at it</u>! Like any skill, becoming more patient takes work. In his best-seller (and excellent read), *Don't Sweat the Small Stuff: and it is all small stuff,* Dr. Carlson discusses the following simple technique to help improve patience.[5]

Dr. Carlson suggests that once you have made the commitment to getting better at patience, you should make it a point to practice patience for at least five minutes a day, everyday. It is likely that you will run into some situation before the day ends that will cause you to be frustrated. Before the day starts, tell yourself that you are not going to react in a negative way during your daily routine, practice, or in a game until you have used up at least five minutes of your patience. Exercising five minutes of patience may be difficult initially because most of us are prone to react in a negative way when we get frustrated. But the more you try, the better you will get, and every minute of improvement will give you confidence in your ability to handle stressful situations. When five minutes becomes easy, shoot for ten—you can never have enough patience! However, it is important to emphasize, that if you do not commit to being patient before the day starts, the probability of it happening will decrease. Developing patience takes work and conscious effort, but once you get better at it, your ability to deal effectively with adversity will increase.

Lesson 4—NEGATIVE PEER PRESSURE

"Don't team up with those who are unbelievers...Therefore, come out from them and separate yourselves from them, says the Lord..." 2 Corinthians 6:14, 17

Who you choose to hang around with will have a significant impact on your life. True friends are gifts from God, and without friends, our lives would be very lonely. It is safe to say that friends are needed, especially when we go through troubled times. However, friends who are not believers can potentially influence you to do things that are not in your best interest.

"Don't team up with those who are unbelievers..." 2 Corinthians 6:14. There will be times in each of our lives, when we will choose to follow the lead of others. People who do not believe in Jesus Christ, do not follow his way. As was emphasized in Section II, Christ has an amazing plan for your life. But if you follow the lead of a nonbeliever, then you will not be following God's righteous plan for you. Take a few moments to think about the people you hang around with and follow. Are they influencing your life in a direction that God would approve?

Always remember that Jesus wants to be your best friend, and he is the best friend you could ever have. Make Jesus the leader of your life. This doesn't necessarily mean that you must always stay away from nonbelievers, but be "separate" from them when it comes to decisions that have important consequences for your life. In fact, if you have a friend who is a nonbeliever, then you may be his or her only chance to believe in Christ. Therefore, don't give up on nonbelievers, and always be ready to tell them about Jesus. However, <u>do not</u> follow their lead! Choose to follow leaders that believe in Christ. It is written that **"[w]hoever walks with the wise will become wise; whoever walks with fools will suffer harm" Proverbs**

13:20. Choose to be wise—choose to follow Jesus Christ and those who believe in him!

Suggested Prayer: "Lord Jesus, thank you for being my best friend. I want to follow your lead. If I am to be influenced by others, let me follow those who believe in you. Please help my friends (list them) who do not believe. Help me to be a friend who can help lead them to you. In your holy name I pray, Amen."

Lesson 5—CRITICISM

"...If God is for us, who can ever be against us?" Romans 8:31

Although nobody likes to fail, all of us will have to deal with failure at some point in our lives—nobody is perfect. One of the reasons we do not like to fail is that we fear criticism. Unfortunately, there are people is this world who are overly critical. In your sporting career, there will be people who will pass judgment on you based on your performance. When you play well, they will claim to be your best friend. When you struggle, they may criticize you and not want anything to do with you. These people typically lack self-esteem and may be trying to develop their own identity through your actions.

Those who really love you will support you when you play well and when you make mistakes. Remember this, <u>Christ will always be your biggest fan</u>, even when you fail! Because you are for Jesus, he is for you. Jesus knows you are not perfect, but loves you anyway. He is the ultimate judge, not people, and he just wants you to just do your best at whatever sport you play.

In 1997, Tony Fernandez, former second baseman for the Cleveland Indians, made an error that contributed to his team losing the World Series. In an interview after the game, Fernandez humbly referred to his belief that everything happens for a reason and that God would help him deal with the consequences of his error. Although Tony received criticism from thousands of people, he was very gracious in keeping his failure in perspective. Never forget,

> **"...If God is for us, who can ever be against us?" Romans 8:31.**

Keep in mind that not all criticism is bad. Some criticism can potentially help you become a better player. Therefore, some criticism you should accept and some you should reject. Determining when criticism should be accepted or rejected is discussed in the application that follows.

APPLICATION—Criticism

Suggested Prayer: "Lord Jesus, help me to deal with criticism. No matter what others think of me, help me to remember that you are for me and love me, even when I do not do my best. Please grant me the wisdom to know when to accept criticism and when to reject it. In your holy name I pray, Amen."

There are several assumptions that can help you deal with criticism. In your notebook, write down each of the following bold-typed statements:

1. "...If God is for us, who can ever be against us?" Romans 8:31

> No matter what happens to you on the playing field, Christ is rooting for you. People's opinions about you are not as important as God's.

2. "Whoever stubbornly refuses to accept criticism will suddenly be broken beyond repair." Proverbs 29:1

> Some criticism is necessary. When criticism is constructive, it can help you become a better player. Do not be stubborn and reject all criticism. Some criticism you should accept and some of it you should reject.

3. "Wounds from a friend are better than many kisses from an enemy." Proverbs 27:6

> Always consider the source doing the criticizing. Does the critic care about your best interest? Although there are caring people in the media, many people who write stories are concerned pri-

marily with whether the story sells and not with whether the criticism helps you or not. As a general rule of thumb, take criticism to heart when it comes from someone who is genuinely interested in your best interest. Ignore criticism if the source does not care about you as a person.

4. Apply constructive criticism to you the player, not you the person.

Don't take criticism home with you—keep it on the playing field. There is more to life than sports. Don't let what others say about you, as an athlete, affect your personal life. If the criticism is constructive, work on it during practice. Commit to enjoying life at home!

Lesson 6—SLUMPING AND REST

"Have mercy on me, LORD, for I am in distress. My sight is blurred because of my tears. My body and soul are withering away. I am dying from grief: my years are shortened by sadness. Misery has drained my strength." Psalm 31:9-10

The above Psalm illustrates how it feels sometimes when things seem to get worse instead of better, no matter how hard you try. It is not uncommon for athletes to experience peaks and valleys throughout the course of a season, as well as during a career. An individual is considered to be in a ***slump*** when a period of a poor performance is evident. Slumping can be caused by a number of physiological and/or psychological factors. A common causal factor that is both physical and mental, but is often overlooked, is lack of rest.

"On the seventh day, having finished his task, God rested from all his work." Genesis 2:2

The above quote from scripture exemplifies the importance of rest. Rest is part of the equation of life. Rest is needed to play your best. People who are in a slump are usually not rested. Understand that rest and sleep are not the same thing. A person that goes to sleep worrying will not rest as well as one who sleeps with a peaceful mind. From a Christian standpoint, rest has to do with renewing your mind, body, and spirit.

"...Come to me, all of you who are weary and carry heavy burdens, and I will give you rest." Matthew 11:28

If you are in a slump, the first thing you need to do is rest. Remember, Jesus is always willing and ready to help those who call on his name—**"God is our refuge and strength, always ready to help in times of trouble" Psalm 46:1.** Before you go to bed at night, tell Jesus about your troubles and ask him to help you deal with them. Ask for rest and a renewed mind, body, and spirit. Then, trust that he will help, and let go of your worries while you sleep. It may take several days of prayer and sleep before you are truly rested. Once you are rested, it is important to focus on other factors that will help you play your best—these factors are discussed in Section IV (Playing in the Zone).

Helpful Scripture: "Why am I discouraged? Why so sad? I will put my hope in God! I will praise him again—my savior and my God!" Psalm 43:5

Lesson 7—INJURIES

Dealing with injuries is one of the most challenging forms of adversity that athletes face. Injuries are unfortunate, but it is important that you know how to deal with them if they come. Of course, always consult with your doctor to determine the severity of the injury, but no matter how severe your injury is, there are some mental techniques that can be applied to any injury situation. First, rest is always essential. Rest with Christ, as was discussed in the previous lesson. Next, an optimistic mindset and hours of rehabilitation are necessary to allow your body to heal optimally. Again, consult with your doctor or doctors regarding your best course of action. Research has demonstrated that during rehabilitation, confidence may decline.[6] Therefore, be prepared to do all you can do to maintain as much of your confidence as you can. Review Section I again and again to help with your confidence.

> "…[W]henever trouble comes your way, let it be an opportunity for joy. For when your faith is tested, your endurance has a chance to grow." James 1:2-3

Remember, it is important to keep in mind that with adversity comes <u>opportunity</u>. Athletes who deal effectively with injuries are often able to perceive benefits from their situation.[7] There are many opportunities that you have when you are injured that you don't have when you are busy as an athlete. Personal growth outside of sports is one opportunity. Write letters to friends and family or read a new book. Remember, Jesus always wants you to make the best of your situation. Do things that you don't get to do when you are busy. Sometimes getting your mind away from sports for a period of time is a good thing because it promotes balance in your life. If you feel anxious and you want to work on something, work on mental-game techniques that can help you get better. Research has demonstrated that three important psychological skills for rehabilitation are goal-setting, positive self-talk, and imagery visualization.[8] These skills will be discussed as they apply to injuries in the application that follows.

APPLICATION—Injuries

Suggested Prayer: "Lord Jesus, please heal my injury. Help me to perceive my injury as an opportunity for growth. Help me to focus on the things that will help facilitate my recovery. Amen."

Goal-setting for an athlete with an injury should be a collaborative effort done with the athlete and his or her doctors. Goals that are important for recovery include: setting a date to return, deciding on the number of times to workout per week, choosing specific range-of-motion goals, setting strength and endurance goals, and making a goal not to overdo it.[9] Remember to write these goals down in your notebook and read them before you start each day of rehabilitation. An emphasis should be made on the last goal, not to overdo it, because overdoing it can irritate the injury and cause a longer and more difficult recovery process. Action is the key, but too much action can be dangerous.

Positive self-talk is also important during rehabilitation. As was previously mentioned, confidence often declines during the rehabilitation process. Be aware of negative self-talk that may intrude into your thinking. Replace negative thoughts such as, "I'm never going to get better" with positive self-talk, like **"…I can do everything with the help of Christ who gives me the strength I need" Philippians 4:13.**

Finally, healing imagery may be beneficial. Take a few minutes each day to visualize your injury actually healing. See the injured body tissue disappearing and new stronger tissue replacing it—do this each day. Although healing imagery may seem a little farfetched, the healing process has been associated with all three of the psychological factors discussed. In one study, athletes that were identified as fast healing (fewer than 5 weeks) used more goal-setting, more positive self-talk strategies, and more healing imagery than slow-healing (more than 16 weeks) athletes.[10] Think as optimistically and opportunistically as you can when you are injured. Have faith in Jesus to heal you, and remember that getting through injuries can <u>build character</u>.

> **For when your faith is tested, your endurance has a chance to grow. So let it grow, for when your endurance is fully developed, you will be strong in character and ready for anything." James 1:3-4**

REVIEW OF MAIN POINTS

1. Understand that adversity is part of life and sports.

   > "Dear friends, don't be surprised at the fiery trials you are going through, as if something strange were happening to you." 1 Peter 4:12

2. See adversity as an opportunity to build character.

   > "[W]henever trouble comes your way, let it be an opportunity for joy. For when your faith is tested, your endurance has a chance to grow. So let it grow, for when your endurance is fully developed, you will be strong in character and ready for anything." James 1:2-4

3. Always pray when you feel worried.

   > "Don't worry about anything, instead, pray about everything. Tell God what you need, and thank him for all he has done. If you do this, you will experience God's peace, which is far more wonderful than the human mind can understand…" Philippians 4:6-7

4. Expect God to answer your prayers in some way.

   > "…when you ask him, be sure that you really expect him to answer, for a doubtful mind is as unsettled as a wave of the sea that is driven and tossed by the wind. People like this should not expect to receive anything from the Lord." James 1:6-7

5. Commit to being patient each day, God's awesome plan for you takes time.

> "Be glad for all God is planning for you. Be patient in trouble, and always be prayerful." Romans 12:12

6. Do not follow those who do not believe in God, lead them.

> "Don't team up with those who are unbelievers...Therefore, come out from them and separate yourselves from them, says the Lord..." 2 Corinthians 6:14, 17

7. God is for you. Accept criticism from those who care about you, ignore critics that don't.

> "...If God is for us, who can ever be against us?" Romans 8:31

> "Whoever stubbornly refuses to accept criticism will suddenly be broken beyond repair." Proverbs 29:1

8. When slumping or injured, rest with Christ. Use your psychological techniques when awake.

> "...Come to me, all of you who are weary and carry heavy burdens, and I will give you rest." Matthew 11:28

> "...I can do everything with the help of Christ who gives me the strength I need." Philippians 4:13

REFERENCES: Dealing with Adversity

1. Crocker, P. (1992). Managing stress by competitive athletes: ways of coping. *International Journal of Sport Psychology*, 23, 161-175.

2. Lazarus, R.S. (1991). Cognition and motivation in emotion. *American Psychologist*, 46, 352-367.

3. Butt, J., Weinberg, R., & Horn, T. (2003). The intensity and directional interpretation of anxiety: fluctuations throughout competition and relationship to performance, *Sport Psychologist*, 17, 35-55.

4. Csikszentmihalyi, M. (1990). *Flow: The psychology of optimal experience.* New York: Harper.

5. Carlson, R. (1997). *Don't Sweat the Small Stuff...and it's All Small Stuff.* New York: Hyperion.

6. Quinn, A.M., & Fallon, B.J. (1999). The changes in psychological characteristics and reactions of elite athletes from injury onset until full recovery. *Journal of Applied Sport Psychology*, 11, 210-229.

7. Udry, E., Gould, D., Bridges, D., & Beck, L. (1997). Down but not out: Athlete responses to season-ending injuries. *Journal of Sport & Exercise Psychology*, 3, 229-248.

8. Petitpas, A., & Danish, S. (1995). Caring for injured athletes. In S. Murphy (Ed.), *Sport psychology interventions* (pp. 255-281). Champaign, IL: Human Kinetics.

9. Theodorakis, Y., Beneca, A., Goudas, M., Panagiotis, A., & Malliou, P. (1996). The effect of personal goals, self-efficacy, and self-satisfaction on injury rehabilitation. *Journal of Sport Rehabilitation*, 5, 214-233.

10. Ievleva, L., & Orlick, T. (1991). Mental links to enhanced healing. *The Sport Psychologist*, 5(1), 25-40.

SECTION IV: PLAYING IN THE ZONE

"Dear brothers and sisters, what's the use of saying you have faith if you don't prove it by your actions?" James 2:14

In order to play your best, you must trust yourself and have faith! There are interesting parallels between how the Bible tells us to live our lives and what is termed "the zone" in athletics. As a Christian, it is important to follow the rules set forth in the Bible. However, just following the written law of God will not get you to heaven—you must also have faith! Similarly in athletics, you will not play your best if you are focused too much on the rules of the task (i.e., technique). Yes, sound technique is needed, but if you lack faith and do not trust yourself at the moment of execution, then you will not be able to perform as athletically as you potentially could. Faith and self-trust as they pertain to athletics will be central topics of focus in this section as well as other important factors associated with playing in the zone.

Although different definitions of ***the zone*** have been set forth by different scholars, each definition typically regards the feelings and/or characteristics that are associated with periods of enhanced performance. The zone is a temporary state in which athletes feel a heightened sense of awareness, and both focus and confidence is greater than what is typical. Concern with failure is minimized and an underlying feeling of enjoyment is often prevalent. Athletes are immersed in the moment and skills seem easy to perform, almost as if they happen automatically. Performing in the zone is what every athlete desires, but unfortunately, it is not always easy to get there.

Although there is no exact formula for how to get into the zone, it is important that you are aware of ways to think and not think that will help you play your best. Successful athletes tend to have high levels of confidence, engage in consistent goal-setting and achieving, and have effective coping skills.[1] Therefore, it is important that you consistently work on the lessons in Sections I-III that deal with each of these characteristics in addition to the lessons in this section. Know that it will take hard work before playing in the zone is even a possibility, but once you get there, things will seem easy if you let faith guide your actions.

Lesson 1: STAY IN THE PRESENT

"...[D]on't worry about tomorrow, for tomorrow will bring its own worries. Today's trouble is enough for today." Matthew 6:34

One of the most important of all sport psychology principles is to <u>stay in the present.</u> When athletes describe their best performances, they invariably report feeling immersed in the present.[2] However, it is not uncommon for athletes to think about the consequences of their performance before it happens. Fear of failure is a factor that can prevent you from playing in the zone. Consider the individual who thinks thoughts such as, "what will my teammates think if I strike out?" or "don't mess up when it counts." With both of these statements, the athlete is looking into the future with a fear of failure. In order to perform your best, it is important for you to focus on the current processes that will help you play effectively in <u>the now</u>. More productive statements are, "if I focus on one shot at a time, the results will be good", or "let's practice today like we want to play tomorrow." These types of statements are more conducive to effective performance in the present and will better prepare you for the impending future.

If you find your mind wandering into the future or thinking about past mistakes, know that focusing on what you need to do <u>right now</u> is essential if you want to play your best. Focus all of your attention on the task at hand and let the results happen as they may. Remember Jesus, who always took care of his business while staying in the present, even though he knew that his future held many difficult trials. He continued to perform miracles and preach about the Kingdom of God even though he knew he would soon be crucified. He focused on doing the right action each moment of each day and trusted in the Lord's future plan for him. So remember, **"...don't**

worry about tomorrow, for tomorrow will bring its own worries. Today's trouble is enough for today" Matthew 6:34. Staying in the present is a key factor to playing in the zone!

APPICATION—Stay in the Present

Suggested prayer: "Lord Jesus, help me not to worry about the future or the past. Help me to trust in you today and to focus on the things in the moment that will help me play as well as I am capable of playing. Help me to do the things that I need to do in order to be successful in your eyes. Amen."

In order to play in the present, there are two areas of your mental-game that need to be sound. First, you must not be afraid to fail. When athletes describe playing in the zone, they talk about being unafraid.[3] Nobody likes to fail, but those who learn to deal with fear effectively have a much better chance of playing their best. People who fear too much are often driven to succeed for the wrong reasons. Winning for some provides a feeling of self-worth. They believe they are better people when they win and worse when they lose. Therefore, the outcome of the game can potentially affect one's self-esteem (i.e., self-worth), which can elicit fear when things are not going well. Remember, Jesus loves you unconditionally! It doesn't matter if you win or lose on the scoreboard. It only matters that you love God and do your best to love others as much as you can. With an attitude characterized by love, you will learn to fear losing less. Never forget that because you believe in Christ you have already won! Remind yourself of this before every game or performance.

The second area of importance in regard to playing in the present is your commitment to your process goals during competition. As discussed in Section II, ***process goals*** are objectives that relate specifically to doing your best during a particular performance. For example, keeping your head down when swinging a baseball bat, or focusing on staying relaxed during a long run. In your notebook, remind yourself of all the process goals that are needed in order for you to play your best. Write them out again. Process goals need to be fresh in your mind before every competition. If you do the things you need to do to be successful, you will be successful. The score of the game will add up on its own. Therefore, don't worry about the outcome while you play—focus on your process goals. Remember, in order to play your best you must <u>stay in the present.</u> Commit to staying in the present before each game and stay focused on your process goals during competition.

Lesson 2—FAITH

"What is faith? It is the confident assurance that what we hope for is going to happen. It is evidence of things we cannot yet see." Hebrews 11:1

Before mastering a particular skill, athletes usually progress through learning stages that have certain characteristics. In the beginning, the learner usually has a high degree of self-awareness and tries to make sense of positioning the body in certain ways in order to perform the particular task. However, once the skill is mastered, athletes are able to produce the appropriate movements with little conscious effort, almost automatically.[4] Think of the first time you learned to ride a bike. You were probably consumed with keeping the handle bars straight, and any slight wobble caused you to panic and focus all of your attention on regaining control. You panicked because you lacked faith. However, later, when you mastered the skill, you were able to ride your bike without thinking about anything or giving it much effort. Your faith improved.

Following their best performances, elite athletes often report that they were not thinking about anything during the execution of the particular skill.[5] The skill just happened automatically, without much effort. Once you have mastered a skill to a certain degree, the key to playing your best is to have faith that what you hope for will happen. For this to occur, you must trust yourself during the execution of your particular skill.[6] Just LET the execution happen. <u>Don't MAKE it happen, LET it happen</u>. Too much control will not allow you to perform in your zone. Remember, because you trust in Christ, you have nothing to lose. Therefore, spread your wings and fly.

> **"But I am trusting you, O LORD saying, "You are my God!" My future is in your hands…" Psalm 31:14-15**

Before performing, make the decision to play with faith and trust. Believe that what you hope for is going to happen, trust yourself, and then LET it happen!

Lesson 3: RULES OF THE TASK

"...[Those] who tried so hard to get right with God by keeping the law, never succeeded. Why not? Because they were trying to get right with God by keeping the law and being good instead of by depending on faith. They stumbled over the great rock in their path." Romans 9:31-32

The Bible emphasizes that being a Christian is not only about trying hard to follow the written laws of scripture. You must also have faith! Similarly, in sport, <u>trying too hard</u> by focusing too much attention on the <u>rules of the task</u> may prevent you from performing your best.[7] Think back to the bicycle example. After you learned to ride your bike effectively, you could just get on it and go, you didn't have to think much, if at all. However, if someone told you to try your hardest to keep the handle bars straight (i.e., rules of the task), you would likely notice that you would not be as fluid—probably a little more "jerky." Kids who know how to ride a bike well might not be able to explain precisely how to ride a bike effectively, but they do trust themselves and do not depend on the rules of the bicycle-task in order to get from home to the playground.

As previously mentioned, athletes who report performing in the zone, usually emphasize letting the action happen automatically. Oftentimes if we are playing poorly, we focus too much on the rules of the task because we do not trust ourselves to get the job done. For example, think of a basketball player who is struggling at the free-throw line. Likely, a struggling free-throw shooter worries too much about technique, such as, bending their knees or keeping their shooting elbow straight. On the other hand, a superior free-throw shooter focuses on seeing the ball go in, trusting his or herself, and then letting it go. Yes, proper technique is very important. However, technique should be focused on and mastered during practice.

SECTION IV: PLAYING IN THE ZONE

Self-trust and faith are needed when the game is played. As with your salvation, if you don't have faith, you won't make it to heaven even if you always do your best to obey the laws of the Bible. Similarly, if you rely too much on technique, and try too hard to control the movement, then you lack faith. Remember, faith is a key component to the zone—trust your technique and execute with faith!

Lesson 4: HARD WORK

"So you see, it isn't enough just to have faith. Faith that doesn't show itself by good deeds is no faith at all—it is dead and useless." James 2:17

Keeping the last two lessons in mind, it is important to emphasize that hard work needs to be "sandwiched" between faith. Although hard work was discussed in Section I, it is such an important aspect to playing your best that it needs to be emphasized again. Without hard work, faith will not get you very far as an athlete. You must start out with some degree of faith, then you need hard work, then you need faith again. First, you need faith in yourself that someday you will become the athlete that you hope to be. If you do not believe in yourself you will never reach your potential. Next, you need hard work! In **Romans 12:11**, Apostle Paul writes, **"[n]ever be lazy in your work, but serve the Lord enthusiastically."** Remember, sports can be a medium to show your belief in Christ. Therefore, work hard in order to shine on the playing field. When you work hard, you get better slowly but surely. At times, you will have to take a step backwards before you take two steps forward, but if you keep working hard, you will get there. Finally, you need faith again. You need to trust that all your hard work will play out when it counts—during your performance!

In the last lesson, it was discussed that focusing too much on technique can prevent you from getting into the zone. But this contradicts the fact that you need effective technique in order to be your best. Understand that you need hard work in practice in order to attain effective technique. A baseball player with a terrible swing <u>cannot</u> just rely on faith as a hitter. As James said, **"...it isn't enough to have faith" James 2:17.** As an athlete, you need to have good deeds to go with your faith. Think of hard work and success in practice as your good deeds related to your sport. Every day that you work hard, you are doing good deeds. When it is game time, it is time to reap the benefits of your hard work—to do this you must trust yourself and have faith!

APPLICATION—Lessons 2-4

Suggested Prayer: "Lord Jesus, thank you for the ability and opportunity to play sports. Help me to know that you are with me when I play. Help me to work hard in practice and trust myself during competition. Let my thoughts be filled with optimism—let my actions be characteristic of faith. Amen."

Remember, hard work is needed before you can play in the zone. Work hard on your technique. During practice, seek feedback from your coaches regarding your technique so that you will know what areas need work. Make a commitment to improve everyday. Once you master the technique of your sport to a reasonable degree, it is then time to trust it and let it happen. As with your salvation, you must give up control to be successful.

> **"Whoever clings to this life will lose it, and whoever loses this life will save it." Luke 17:33**

As a Christian, you know that you cannot save your own life, only Jesus can. You must give up control of your life to him in order to make it to heaven. Therefore, in a paradoxical way, you gain control by giving up control, because going to heaven is what we all want to achieve. Apply this way of thinking to your sport. Although it seems counterintuitive, once you master your technique to a reasonable degree, the less you try to control the movement, the more fluid it will be. In other words, the more you give up control, the more you will gain control.

The concept of giving up control is very difficult for some athletes to understand and apply. We all like to be in control of our situation, so it is a challenge to give it up. Know that you will need to trust yourself during the execution of a skill in order to give up conscious control of a particular movement. A preperformance routine can help with this objective.

A *preperformance routine* is consistent, systematic pattern of action and thoughts that has a purpose of fostering self-trust, attentional focus, and ultimately performance.[8] Preperformance routines are especially helpful for *self-paced tasks*—tasks that allow a reasonable amount of time for the athlete to prepare and initiate a particular skill.[9] Examples of self-paced tasks include sports such as golf, bowling, and diving, or skills like pitching, free-throw shooting, field-goal kicking, or serving a tennis or volleyball.

An effective preperformance routine should have several components that serve specific purposes. First, an athlete should prepare his or herself in a consistent and effective way. Use the same steps every time before executing the skill. For example, a free-throw shooter in basketball might put one foot slightly in front of the other, bounce the ball a couple of times, and bend his or her knees before preparing to shoot. Consistent preparation serves to get the body ready for action and helps to keep one's focus on the task at hand. Mental imagery is also a helpful aspect of the preparation stage. It is helpful for the free-throw shooter to see and feel the ball going into the net with perfect trajectory. As discussed in Section I, imagery serves to foster optimism as well as to prime the body for the impending skill. Imagery can be used before or after the physical preparatory steps, depending on which order is more comfortable for the individual.

Next is the execution phase. During the execution of the skill, the mind should be as "quiet" as possible.[10] For example, you should not be giving yourself instructions on how to shoot (e.g., keep elbow straight, flick wrist, etc.). Instead, focus your attention on something external, such as the front of the rim. Focusing on something external can help reduce distraction (e.g., crowd noise) and help take your attention away from the mechanics of the technique or movement (i.e., promotes a quiet mind). Make sure your focus on the external cue is soft. That is, <u>do not</u> focus too intensely. Then, just <u>let it</u> happen. With your attention on the external cue, trust yourself and let your body take over.

A preperformance routine gives you a sense of control over the situation even though you must give up control at the moment of execution. When you do the same thing over and over again and are successful, you will develop confidence in yourself and the sequence of steps in your routine. Remember, the key is self-trust. Adam Vineterri, a place-kicker in the NFL, incorporates Christ into his thinking in order to help him give up control and enhance self-trust. He reminds himself that Jesus is with him before he kicks. Adam's technique is apparently effective; he kicked the winning field goal in the final seconds of two different Super Bowls!

If you participate in a sport in which you perform a self-paced task, write in your notebook what you think would be an effective preperformance routine based on the techniques discussed thus far. Remember to include: consistent preparation, imagery, and a soft focus on an external cue. Most importantly, emphasize a trusting mindset and commit to <u>letting it happen</u>. It will take some time before you will develop confidence in your routine; but eventually, it will seem automatic and you will not have to give it much thought. When you reach the point of not having to think much, your chances of performing in <u>the zone</u> will increase.

If you participate in a sport that consists of externally-paced tasks, then a different approach to the preperformance routine is needed. ***Externally-paced tasks*** are events that are reactive in nature and require anticipating an opponent's intentions (e.g., soccer, boxing, ice hockey, to name a few).[11] Preperformance routines can also be used with externally paced tasks, but are limited primarily to <u>pregame</u> situations. Rituals should include behaviors that promote physical readiness and mental optimism. Prayer, positive imagery, and consistent warm-up routines can be effective components to a pre-game routine for externally-paced tasks. During competition, the key is to anticipate with faith and react with self-trust. Remember, Christ is with you. No matter what sport you play, it is important that you learn to trust your instincts and then let it happen. Remind yourself to have fun while you are at it. Having fun is also a characteristic of playing in the zone and will be discussed in greater length in the lesson that follows.

Lesson 5—ENJOY THE MOMENT

"Always be full of joy in the Lord. I say it again—rejoice." Philippians 4:4

One of the most underemphasized characteristics of performing in the zone is the feeling of enjoyment while performing a particular skill. Optimal performance states are often characterized by pleasant feelings or even exhilaration with no concern of external rewards because performing the skill itself is intrinsically rewarding.[12] In other words, just doing the particular skill feels good and brings a certain degree of happiness, so the performer is not as concerned with the consequences of the performance.

Many athletes are only happy if they are winning or doing well. Nobody likes to lose or play poorly, but try your best not to let the scoreboard dictate how you will feel during your competition. Know that after you have done your "good deeds" by working hard during practice, as discussed in Lesson 4 of this Section, you then deserve some fun. However, you must give yourself <u>permission</u> to have some. In the Bible, it is written that there is **"[a] time to cry and a time to laugh. A time to grieve and a time to dance" Ecclesiastes 3:4.** In sports, when it is game time, it is time to dance!

Many people think that if you have fun while playing sports then you are not serious about winning. This is far from the truth. Understand that the more you are able to enjoy your sport and the process of competing, the more likely you will be able to get into your zone and achieve optimal performance. And let us not forget, Christ wants you to enjoy what you are doing! Make the decision before you play to "rejoice in the Lord" and commit to having fun. In addition to the good feelings it brings, having fun can help get you in the zone!

APPLICATION—Enjoy the Moment

Helpful Scripture: "You have turned my mourning into joyful dancing. You have taken away my clothes of mourning and clothed me with joy, that I might sing praises to you and not be silent. O LORD my God, I will give you thanks forever!" Psalm 30:11-12

Before your next performance, commit to having fun. First, thank the Lord for giving you the ability and opportunity to play sports. Ask him to be with all of the competitors, to keep everyone safe, and to help everyone enjoy the competition. Next, approach your performance as if you have already won before it starts. That is, think of all the hard work you have put into your sport as the victory. All that is left to be done is to dance! It doesn't matter if you dance well or not, the only thing you have to do is to leave every move you have on the dance floor. To really have fun when you dance, you cannot evaluate every step you take while you are dancing. If you do, you will not be very graceful. You have to trust yourself and let it happen—just go with the flow of the music. There will be plenty of time to evaluate your performance constructively when the dance is over.

> "...[A]nyone who becomes as humble as this little child is the greatest in the Kingdom of Heaven." Matthew 18:4

Children do not have much pride or worry too much about making mistakes when they are on the dance floor. When children dance, their sole priority is to have fun. There are many references about becoming more like a child in the Bible. Endorsing the concept of dancing like a child when you compete can help you play your best. When you perform, be like a child and do <u>not</u> worry about the outcome of your performance. Instead, focus on the things that you need to do to make you successful. That is, focus on your *process goals* that were emphasized in Lesson 1 to help you <u>stay in the present</u>. Your process goals will be the blueprint for your dance moves. Be creative and trust your instincts like a child would—the more you are able to dance like a child, the better chance you have of playing your best!

REVIEW OF MAIN POINTS

1. Stay in the present!

> "...[D]on't worry about tomorrow, for tomorrow will bring its own worries. Today's trouble is enough for today." Matthew 6:34

2. Have faith and trust yourself before and during the execution of your particular skill.

> "What is faith? It is the confident assurance that what we hope for is going to happen. It is evidence of things we cannot yet see." Hebrews 11:1

3. Once you have mastered a skill, don't depend too much on the rules of the task (i.e., technique). Trust yourself and <u>let</u> it happen.

> "...[Those] who tried so hard to get right with God by keeping the law, never succeeded. Why not? Because they were trying to get right with God by keeping the law and being good instead of by depending on faith. They stumbled over the great rock in their path." Romans 9:31-32

4. Hard work is a prerequisite to peak performance. Conceptualize hard work and success during practice as "good deeds."

> "So you see, it isn't enough just to have faith. Faith that doesn't show itself by good deeds is no faith at all—it is dead and useless." James 2:17

> "Never be lazy in your work, but serve the Lord enthusiastically." Romans 12:11

5. Have fun—when it is game time, dance like a child!

> "Always be full of joy in the Lord. I say it again—rejoice." Philippians 4:4

> "...[A]nyone who becomes as humble as this little child is the greatest in the Kingdom of Heaven." Matthew 18:4

REFERENCES: Playing in the Zone

1. Williams, J.M., & Krane, V. (2001). Psychological characteristics of peak performance. In J.M. William (Ed.), *Applied Sport Psychology: Personal Growth to Peak Performance* (4th ed.). Mountain View, CA: Mayfield Publishing.

2. Ravizza, K. (1984). Qualities of the peak experience in sport. In J.M. Silva & R.S. Weinberg (Eds.), *Psychological Foundations of Sport* (pp. 452-462). Champaign, IL: Human Kinetics.

3. Jackson, S.A. (1996). Toward a conceptual understanding of the flow experience in elite athletes. *Research Quarterly for Exercise and Sport, 67*, 76-90.

4. Rose, D.J. (1997). *A Multilevel Approach to the Study of Motor Control and Learning. Needham Heights*, MA: Allyn & Bacon.

5. Ravizza (1977). Peak experiences in sport. *Journal of Humanistic Psychology, 17*, 35-40.

6. Moore, W.E., & Stevenson, J.R. (1991). Understanding trust in the performance of complex automatic sport skills. *The Sport Psychologist, 5*, 281-289.

7. Masters, R.S.W. (1992). Knowledge, nerves and know-how: The role of explicit versus implicit knowledge in the breakdown of complex motor skill under pressure. *British Journal of Psychology, 83*, 343-358.

8. Boutcher, S.H., & Rotella, R.J. (1987). A psychological skills educational program for closed-skill performance enhancement. *The Sport Psychologist*, 1, 127-137.

9-11. Singer, R.N. (2000). Performance and human factors: Considerations about cognition and attention for self-paced and externally-paced events. *Ergonomics*, 43, 1661-1680.

12. Csikszentmihalyi, M. (1990). *Flow: The psychology of optimal experience*. New York: Harper.

SECTION V: TEAMWORK

"Just as our bodies have many parts and each part has a special function, so it is with Christ's body. We are all parts of his one body, and each of us has different work to do. And since we are all one body in Christ, we belong to each other, and each of us needs all the others." Romans 12:4-5

If you play team sports, this final section is of utmost importance. To be the best team player you can be, it is imperative that you have the right approach and attitude towards the concept of teamwork. Themes of teamwork are discussed in a number of places in the Bible and many of the lessons can be applied to sports. As with the Christian body, teammates have different roles in making the team as effective as it can be. A key part of teamwork is that each teammate <u>needs all the others</u>. Although conflict within a team is probably inevitable, it is essential that individuals learn to set aside personal differences and work together on the things that need to be done in order to maximize the potential of the team.

"Then make me truly happy by agreeing wholeheartedly with each other, loving one another, and working together with one heart and purpose." Philippians 2:2

<u>Working together with one heart and purpose</u> should be a primary objective for every team member. You cannot be too concerned with satisfying your own personal objectives. Be aware of your own selfish ambition and do not be jealous of your teammates. Know that when your teammates succeed, you succeed, and vice versa. Your happiness should be a result of you doing your part to make your team the best it can be. It is important that you commit to developing a serving mindset. Consistently ask yourself, "How can I serve my team?" One way is to be concerned with the welfare of your teammates and coaches and always offer them respect. Throughout this section, more examples will be given regarding the principles of effective teamwork. As you read the individual lessons and applications, remember that each teammate <u>needs all the others</u>. You need Jesus the most. Stay close to him and he will show you how to be the best team player you can be.

Lesson 1—SERVE YOUR TEAM, NOT YOURSELF

"For even I, the Son of Man, came here not to be served but to serve others, and to give my life as a ransom for many." Mark 10:45

There is no bigger team player in the history of the world than Jesus Christ. During his human life, Jesus did not seek glory as we often do; he sought to serve others. He was always ready to do what he needed to do to help his teammates (us) and his team (The Kingdom of God). Although he was and is the King of Kings, he was always humble and always serving. In fact, he washed the feet of his disciples as his impending crucifixion grew near. Jesus' purpose was to serve others and then die for us so that our sins would be forgiven. Although his motive was not to receive glory, he now sits at the right hand of The Father and lives in glory forever. Jesus Christ is the Savior of the World!

Although we can never be as great as Jesus, we can adopt his serving attitude. If you play team sports, it is important to be focused on serving your team, not yourself. Know that an awareness of your own progress (i.e., personal statistics) is not necessarily negative. In fact, assessing your own progress can be a positive behavior when it motivates you to be better. However, make sure that your priorities are in order. Remember, as a member of a team you are a small part of a bigger picture. Your primary motive should <u>not</u> be to make your statistics better; it should be to contribute to your team.

If you work hard to serve your team and your team is successful, you will be happy with your individual statistics because they will be the result of team-focused hard work. Work hard to serve your team, and your efforts will be rewarded accordingly.

"The one who plants and the one who waters work as a team with the same purpose. Yet they will be rewarded individually, according to their own hard work." 1 Corinthians 3:8

APPLICATION—Serve Your Team, Not Yourself

Suggested Prayer: "Heavenly Father, help me to be focused on serving my team. Let my statistics be a result of hard work driven by the desire to be the best team player I can be. Amen."

Basketball legend Magic Johnson did everything he could to help his team win. As a result, his Los Angeles Lakers of the 1980s were some of the best teams in the history of the NBA. Magic's stats were great, but statistics were not his primary concern. His focus was to do whatever he could to help his team win championships and passing to his teammates was his first option. His consistent passing made him the all-time leader in assists for many years, the league MVP three times, and an all-star for twelve seasons. More importantly, his team won five NBA championships! Magic served his team admirably and his impressive statistics were a result of his serving mindset.

Take a few moments to reflect on the degree to which you are currently serving your team. Imagine that you are in a court of law and are being judged on whether you have served your team admirably or not. What would you tell the judge or jury in your defense that supports the argument that you put your team first? Think of the specific actions that you have taken in the past year that would substantiate your case. Take as much time as you need.

Next, think of the prosecutor discussing all of the times that you put yourself first, ahead of your team. The prosecutor in this case is God, so he knows all the times you put yourself first. He knows how you interpret the importance of your statistics, he knows everything. How would this case turn out? Could you do a good job of defending yourself?

If you know for sure that you would lose the case, don't worry, just know that a change in your motives and actions is needed and that you still have time. In your notebook, list as many ways that you can think of in which you can serve your team. You can serve your team both on and off the playing field. Take your time, if you can't think of many reasons now, know that more ways will come to mind in the future as long as you are committed to having a serving attitude. Remember, you are a small but significant part of a bigger picture. Make the decision to play for the bigger picture!

Lesson 2—UNDERSTANDING AND ACCEPTING YOUR ROLE ON THE TEAM

"God has given each of us the ability to do certain things well.….If you are a teacher, do a good job of teaching. If your gift is to encourage others, do it! If you have money, share it generously. If God has given you leadership ability, take the responsibility seriously. And if you have a gift for showing kindness to others, do it gladly." Romans 12:6-8

In order to be successful with team sports, it is imperative that each member understands his or her role on the team and is committed to doing the things necessary to contribute to the success of the team.[1] Each team member has different gifts and it is important that you accept your role in how you will contribute to the success of your team. Know that some members of the team will receive more credit for the team's success than others. The quarterback of a football team will likely receive more glory than an offensive lineman following big wins. The center of a basketball team will usually be interviewed after the game before the "sixth" man who gets less playing time. And the clean-up hitter of a baseball team will get more at bats during the season than a pinch-hitter.

> "All the believers were of one heart and mind, and they felt that what they owned was not their own; they shared everything they had." Acts 4:32

No matter what your role is, it is important to know that you are a co-owner of your team. What you own, your teammates own, and what they own, you own. Regardless of what specific role each player has on the team, all that really matters is that your team becomes as good as it can be and that you do your role to make it happen. When your teammates are successful, then you are successful, and when you succeed, they succeed. If you are a star on the team, always give credit to your teammates first. Similarly, if you play a lesser role, always be happy for the success of a teammate who has a larger role. Without each other, the stars on the team and those that come off the bench will never play for a team that realizes its potential. Whatever your role is or becomes, accept it graciously and serve your team admirably.

APPLICATION: Understanding and Accepting Your Role on the Team

Suggested Prayer: "Lord Jesus, help me to understand and accept my role on the team. Let myself and each of my teammates think of each other as co-owners of our team and let us each do our part to make our team be the best it can be. Amen."

To understand your role on your team, it is first important to know the mission of the team. If your team doesn't have a mission statement, suggest to your coach that your team needs one. A *mission statement* is the ultimate quest that provides the underlying motivation of a team giving purpose and direction for why you play. In your notebook, write out what you think your role is on the team. If your team already has a mission statement, discuss your role with respect to the mission. When you get the opportunity, be sure to discuss what you have written with your coach. It is important that you are both on the same page about your role.

Although each team member will have a different role to some degree, it is crucial that you assess the importance of each teammate's role in a Christian way. In your notebook, do your best to draw a bicycle wheel, with an outer tire and rim with spokes connecting to the inner hub. Draw one spoke for each member of your team including yourself. See your team in terms of the bicycle wheel, and <u>see yourself and your teammates each as a spoke on the wheel</u>. If you own a bike, you probably know that if any of the spokes break, the wheel (i.e., team) can still function, but it will <u>not</u> function as effectively as it would if all of the spokes were strong. Each of the spokes is equally important and no spoke deserves any more credit for a smooth ride than any of the other spokes.

> **"For the whole law can be summed up in this one command: 'Love your neighbor as yourself.' But if instead of showing love among yourselves you are always biting and devouring one another, watch out! Beware of destroying one another." Galatians 5:14-15**

Always try to <u>love your teammates as yourself</u>. As with the bicycle spokes analogy, consider yourselves as equals and always do your best to treat each other with respect. Know that inner-team conflict is probably inevitable, and will have to be dealt with from time to time, but conflict can be minimized if you approach team sports with a Christian attitude. How to deal with team conflict if it manifests is discussed in the lesson that follows.

Lesson 3—COHESION VERSES CONFLICT

"Now, dear brothers and sisters, I appeal to you by the authority of the Lord Jesus Christ to stop arguing among yourselves. Let there be real harmony so there won't be divisions in the church [i.e., team]. I plead with you to be of one mind, united in thought and purpose." 1 Corinthians 1:10

Team conflict is one aspect of team sports that is very difficult to avoid. It is probably safe to say that all teams have had, have, or will have some degree of team conflict at some point during a season. Conflict can be potentially detrimental to the team if it negatively affects cohesion. *Cohesion* refers to the dynamic process of a team sticking together and staying united in pursuit of specific objectives.[2] Cohesion is described as "dynamic" because it is a process that is constantly evolving. For some teams, cohesion gets better as the season goes on, for other teams cohesion gets worse. Cohesion is needed for a team to reach its potential. Individuals do not always have to get along perfectly with each other in order to be successful, but it is important that when it is game time, each individual on the team is <u>united in thought and purpose.</u>

There are many factors that can cause team conflict and ultimately minimize cohesion and team effectiveness. Conflict should be avoided when possible, and dealt with quickly when it appears. To avoid and deal with conflict effectively, and to promote cohesion, adhere to the following three guidelines:

1. Be a good listener.

> "Dear friends, be quick to listen, slow to speak, and slow to get angry." James 1:19

Clear communication is an important aspect of team cohesion and can alleviate many team problems.[3] Make it a point to listen more than you talk. If God wanted you to talk more than listen, he would have given you two mouths and one ear!

2. Respect your teammates.

> **"Show respect for everyone..." 1 Peter 2:17**

We all desire to be respected by others. Don't ever look down on your teammates. When teammates choose not to respect each other, they unknowingly reduce cohesiveness.

3. Don't let jealousy and selfish ambition be a part of you.

> **"For wherever there is jealousy and selfish ambition, there you will find disorder and every kind of evil." James 3:16**

Remember, you are a co-owner of your team. When your teammates succeed, you succeed. Always serve your team and be happy for the individual success any of your teammates may receive.

APPLICATION—Cohesion Versus Conflict

Suggested Prayer: "Lord Jesus, help me to be a team player committed to reducing conflict and increasing cohesion on the team. Help me to be a good listener and show respect for my teammates. Keep me from being jealous of my teammates and prevent selfish ambition from being part of me. Amen."

To help with the objectives in the above prayer, practice the following techniques:

1. If problems arise between you and a teammate, try to solve them among yourselves first.

> **"If you are on the way to court and you meet your accuser, try to settle the matter before it reaches the judge..." Luke 12:58**
>
> No one likes a tattletale. Instead of going straight to your coach about a problem that you may have with one of your teammates, confront them in a tactful way. This can be done by "sandwiching" the negative issue between positive points.[4] For example, first tell them that you respect them as a teammate and friend. Then express the problem that you may have with them in as calm a manner as you can. Finally, finish with something positive, such as mentioning the importance of the team goals that you both have. In some cases, your coach will need to be included, but make it a point to try and solve teammate problems among yourselves first.

2. If you are wronged by a teammate, <u>do not</u> pay them back.

> **"Never pay back evil for evil to anyone. Do things in such a way that everyone can see you are honorable. Do your part to live in peace with everyone, as much as possible." Romans 12:17-18**

A player that seeks "pay back" when he or she is wronged by another teammate is only hurting the team. Evil for evil is a dangerous cycle. Do your best to be a forgiving person. Let your teammate know that you do not appreciate what they did, but <u>do not</u> pay back evil with evil.

3. Show a sincere interest in your teammates.

> **"Don't think only about your affairs, but be interested in others, too, and what they are doing." Philippians 2:4**

Make an effort to get to know each of your teammates. Friends are more likely to make cohesive teammates. Make it a goal to compliment your teammates as often as possible. When you are successful, always give credit to your teammates first.

Lesson 4—PLAYER/COACH RELATIONSHIP

"Obey your leaders and submit to their authority. They keep watch over you as men who must give an account. Obey them so that their work will be a joy, not a burden, for that would be of no advantage to you." Hebrews 13:17

Your coach is the leader of your team. In order to be the best team player you can be, it is important that you submit to the authority of your coach. A coach's job is very challenging. A coach has to manage different players with different personalities. The coach has to try and keep everyone as happy as possible, while making decisions based on the best interest of the team. It is important that you have the right attitude towards your coach and respect his or her decisions even if you do not always agree with them. When players and coaches are disrespectful of each other, team cohesion is weakened and the potential of the team suffers. Be a player who is committed to listening and obeying your coach.

"Dear friends, be quick to listen, slow to speak, and slow to get angry. Your anger can never make things right in God's sight." James 1:19-20

Although your coaches will not always say what you want to hear, do your best not to get upset or angry at their statements, particularly when a coach evaluates your performance. How a coach evaluates the performance of a player can affect the player's self-perception of competence.[5] Therefore, your interpretation of a coach's evaluation is very important. Try to view the sport you are playing as a job, and your coach is the CEO. A good CEO balances criticism with praise. However, don't expect praise when you play well, just be thankful when it comes. When a coach criticizes you, interpret the criticism in a positive light, because the purpose of the criticism is to make you and your team better. Have a business relationship with your coach when you take the field. No matter how good or bad your relationship is with your coach off the field, do not take personally any type of criticism that is offered while playing. Remember, **"(w)ounds from a friend are better than many kisses from an enemy" Proverbs 27:6.** Criticism can make you a better player. Listen to your coach and do your best to obey.

APPLICATION—Player/Coach Relationship

Suggested Prayer: "Lord Jesus, help me to respect and obey the authority of my coach. Help me to be a good listener and to interpret criticism in a positive light. Amen."

In your notebook, draw two big circles next to each other. In one circle write, "*player/coach personal relationship.*" In the other circle write, "*player/coach business relationship.*" Notice that the only difference between the two circles is the word "business" or "personal." Although it is often difficult to tell the difference between the two, every player has a personal and business relationship with their coach. Any type of interaction with your coach that has to do with bettering the team and/or yourself has to do with your business relationship with your coach. Any player/coach interaction that has to do with friendship has to do with your personal relationship. Whenever you take the field, whether it is in practice or a game, it is important that you interpret your interaction with your coach from a business perspective.

To be the best team player you can be, it is important that you have an effective business relationship with your coach. It is likely that you will have better personal relationships with some coaches more than others, but you can have an effective business relationship with all of your coaches. In the "business" circle, write the following words: "*LISTEN, OBEY,* and *RESPECT.*" The more you are able to listen, obey, and respect your coach, the better your business relationship will be. Also write: "*CONSTRUCTIVE CRITICISM.*" Again, always try to accept criticism in a positive light and interpret criticism from a business standpoint. Criticism can help you become a better player. However, criticism can be detrimental if you take things too personally. Athletes who take things too personally may become afraid to make mistakes. As you previously learned, you cannot play your best if you are afraid to make mistakes. Therefore, from a business standpoint, accept criticism from your coach as an important part of making you a better athlete. You will find that if you do the things you need to do to have an effective <u>business</u> relationship with your coach, your <u>personal</u> relationship will also be good. Remember, as a team member your primary goal is to be the best team player you can be. How good a team player you become will depend, in part, on the business relationship that you have with your coach.

REVIEW OF MAIN POINTS

1. Serve your team not yourself!

> "For even I, the Son of Man, came here not to be served but to serve others, and to give my life as a ransom for many." Mark 10:45

2. Every member of a team has a special role.

> "God has given each of us the ability to do certain things well....If you are a teacher, do a good job of teaching. If your gift is to encourage others, do it! If you have money, share it generously. If God has given you leadership ability, take the responsibility seriously. And if you have a gift for showing kindness to others, do it gladly." Romans 12:6-8

3. You are a co-owner of your team. When your teammate succeeds you succeed, and vice versa.

> "All the believers were of one heart and mind, and they felt that what they owned was not their own; they shared everything they had." Acts 4:32

4. Minimize conflict and maximize cohesion.

> "Now, dear brothers and sisters, I appeal to you by the authority of the Lord Jesus Christ to stop arguing among yourselves. Let there be real harmony so there won't be divisions in the church [i.e., team]. I plead with you to be of one mind, united in thought and purpose." 1 Corinthians 1:10

5. Be a good listener. Clear communication is an important aspect of team cohesion.

> **"Dear friends, be quick to listen, slow to speak, and slow to get angry." James 1:19**

6. Respect your teammates and coaches.

> **"Show respect to everyone…" 1 Peter 2:17**

7. Don't let jealousy and selfish ambition be a part of you.

> **"For wherever there is jealousy and selfish ambition, there you will find disorder and every kind of evil." James 3:16**

8. If problems arise between you and a teammate, try to solve problems among yourselves first.

> **"If you are on the way to court and you meet your accuser, try to settle the matter before it reaches the judge…" Luke 13:58**

9. If you are wronged by a teammate, confront them tactfully, <u>do not</u> pay them back.

> **"Never pay back evil for evil to anyone. Do things in such a way that everyone can see you are honorable. Do your part to live in peace with everyone, as much as possible." Romans 12:17**

10. Show a sincere interest in your teammates.

> **"Don't think only about your affairs, but be interested in others, too, and what they are doing." Philippians 2:4**

11. Obey and listen to your coach.

> **"Obey your leaders and submit to their authority…" Hebrews 13:17**

12. Don't take criticism from your coach personally. Accept criticism from a business standpoint and know that criticism can help make you a better player.

> **"Wounds from a friend are better than many kisses from an enemy." Proverbs 27:6**

REFERENCES: Teamwork

1. Paskevich, D.M. Eastabrooks, P.A., Brawley, L.R., & Carron, A.V. (2001). Group cohesion in sport and exercise In R.N. Singer, H.A. Hausenblas, & C.M. Janelle (Eds.), *Handbook of Sport Psychology*, 2nd ed. (pp. 472-494). New York: John Wiley & Sons.

2. Carron, A.V. (1982). Cohesiveness in sport groups: Interpretations and considerations. *Journal of Sport Psychology*, 7, 244-267.

3. Orlick, T. (1990). *In Pursuit of Excellence*. Champaign, IL: Leisure Press.

4. Janssen, J. (1999). *Championship Team Building*. Tucson, AZ: Winning the Mental Game.

5. Smoll, F.L., & Smith, R.E. (2001). Conducting sport psychology training programs for coaches: cognitive-behavioral principles and techniques. In J.M. Williams (Ed.), *Applied Sport Psychology: Personal Growth to Peak Performance,* 4th ed. (pp. 378-400). Mountain View, CA: Mayfield Publishing.

CONCLUSION

"...And let us run with endurance the race that God has set before us. We do this by keeping our eyes on Jesus, on whom our faith depends from start to finish." Hebrews 12:1-2

In order to have a strong mental-game you must have mental endurance. Do not expect that one reading of this book will make you mentally strong. Working on your mental-game should be a continuing process. Although this book can help, the most important book you can reference is the Holy Bible. Understand that if you don't work your mind and spirit they will become weak, as do muscles if they are not exercised. Make Jesus Christ your workout partner and follow his plan for you. He is the most important aspect of your mental-game. Without Jesus in your life, you will never be truly fulfilled no matter how much success you may have in sports.

> **"Follow the Lord's rules for doing his work, just as an athlete either follows the rules or is disqualified and wins no prize." 2 Timothy 2:5**

Many of the rules for a sound mental-game are in this book. To be the best Christian athlete you can be, it is important that you play with confidence, but only to the degree that Christ would approve. Commit to working hard each day and play with passion and desire to achieve the goals you set along the way. Know that in order to play in the zone the key is self-trust, but remember, some days will go your way and some days will not. When adversity comes your way turn to Jesus and know that <u>you will endure.</u> Finally, commit to being a team player. As a Christian, you are a member of the Christian body. Serve your team admirably.

There are thousands of current and former athletes who are soldiers for Christ: David Robinson, Julius Erving, Deion Sanders, Andy Pettitte, Jeff Gordon, Kurt Warner, Reggie White, and the list goes on. Although there are many Christian athletes out there, we need more soldiers to spread the Good News. Hopefully, the lessons of this book will help make you a better athlete, but more importantly, will help you play your sport in a way that will bring glory to Christ in some way. Always remember, no matter whether you win or lose in sports, Jesus Christ will always love you and is always with you. Stay close to him and you will succeed in sports and in life. May God bless you as you play!

GLOSSARY—Sport Psychology Terms

Cognitive anxiety—the phenomenon of worrying about one's impending performance

Cohesion—the dynamic process of a team sticking together and staying united in pursuit of specific objectives

External locus of control—the belief that little or no relationship exists between what one does and the outcome of a given situation

Externally-paced tasks—tasks that require anticipating an opponent's intentions (e.g, soccer, boxing, or football)

Extrinsic motivation—the motive to do something for the purpose of some external result (e.g., winning, earning money or rewards, etc.)

Goal-setting—establishing an objective or objectives that relate to some level of proficiency for a given pursuit

Internal locus of control—the belief that one's actions have a direct relationship to a given outcome

Intrinsic motivation—the motive to do something because it is inherently rewarding (e.g., fun, challenging, etc.)

Mental imagery—the act of seeing and/or feeling the act that you hope to perform before actually performing it

Mission statement—the purpose or ultimate quest that provides the underlying motivation for an individual or team to participate in some activity

Modeling—observing the actions of someone else and then attempting to repeat the movements

Motivation—the factors related to why an individual starts and persists at some activity

Outcome goals—goals that focus on outplaying/outdoing an opponent and/or opponents (e.g., winning a race or a championship)

Performance goals—goals that represent personal improvement (e.g., running a 6:45 mile)

Preperformance routine—a systematic pattern of action and thoughts that can aid athletic performance

Process goals—objectives that relate specifically to doing your best during a particular performance (e.g., keeping your head down while swinging a baseball bat)

Self-confidence—the general belief that one has the ability to perform successfully

Self-paced tasks—tasks that allow a reasonable amount of time for the athlete to prepare and initiate a particular skill (e.g., golf, free-throw in basketball, or a serve in tennis or volleyball)

Self-talk—how you talk to yourself before, during, and after performance

Situational favorableness—the belief that the breaks of a sporting situation are going or will eventually go in your favor

Slump—a period of a poor performance

Somatic anxiety—the interpretation of physical symptoms

The zone—the feelings and/or characteristics that are associated with a heightened state of focus in the moment, confidence, enjoyment, effortless control, and enhanced performance

0-595-32833-4

Printed in the United States
22858LVS00001B/43